Solving Garden Problems
Flowers

Complete Gardener's Library™

SOLVING GAR
FLO

DEN PROBLEMS WERS

A. Cort
Sinnes

National Home
Gardening Club
Minnetonka, Minnesota

Solving Garden Problems—Flowers

Printed in 2005.

Tom Carpenter
Creative Director

Julie Cisler
Book Design & Production

Michele Teigen
Senior Book Development Coordinator

Gina Germ
Photo Editor

4567/08 07 06 05
ISBN 1-58159-053-9
©1999 National Home Gardening Club

National Home Gardening Club
12301 Whitewater Drive
Minnetonka, Minnesota 55343
www.gardeningclub.com

CONTENTS

A Walk in the Garden 7

CHAPTER 1

AVOIDING PROBLEMS: THE BASICS 8

Soil Preparation 10
Water 12
Fertilizers 14
The Right Plant in the
  Right Place 18
Resistant Varieties 20
Animals—The Big Pests 22
A Balanced Approach 30

CHAPTER 2

QUICK-SOLUTION CHART 36

Aphids 38
Aster Yellows 38
Bacterial Soft Rot 38
Bacterial Wilt 39
Basal Rot 39
Black Spot 39
Black Stem Rot 40
Blister Beetle 40
Bristly Rose Slugs 40
Brown Canker 40
Bud Rot and Canna Rot 41
Bulb Mites 41
Bulb Rot 41
Burdock Borers 41
Cabbage Loopers 42
Caterpillars 42
Cercospora Leaf Spot 42
Colorado Potato Beetles 43
Columbine Borers 43
Common Stalk Borer 43
Crown Galls 44
Cutworms 44
Damping Off 44
Diamondback Moths 45
Didymellina Leaf Spot 45
Downy Mildew 45
Earwigs 45

European Corn Borers 46
Fall Web Worms 46
Four Lined Plant Bugs 46
Foxglove Anthracnose 46
Fuller Rose Beetles 47
Fusarium Bulb Rot 47
Fusarium Wilt 47
Fusarium Yellows 47
Gladiolus Thrips 48
Grasshoppers 48
Gray Mold 49
Iris Borer 49
Iron Deficiency 49
Japanese Beetles 50
Lace Bugs 50
Leafhoppers 51
Leaf Miners 51
Leaf Roller 51
Leaf Scorch 52
Leaf Spot 52
Mealy Bugs 52
Mosaic Virus 53
Narcissus Streak 53
Oedema 53
Phlox Plant Bugs 53
Phytophthora Blight 54
Powdery Mildew 54
Root Nematodes 54
Root Rot 54
Rose Budworms 55
Rose Leaf Curl 55
Rose Midges 55
Rose Mosaic 55
Rust 56
Scale 56
Slugs and Snails 56
Spider Mites 57
Spittle Bug 57
Stem Rot 57
Tarnished Plant Bugs 57
Tobacco Budworms 58
Tomato Hornworms 58
Tulip Breaking Virus 58
Verticillium Wilt 58
Violet Sawflies 59
Weevils 59
Whiteflies 59

CHAPTER 3

ENCYCLOPEDIA OF PLANTS 60

Achillea/Yarrow 62

Ageratum/Flossflower 62
Alcea/Hollyhock 64
Anemone/Anemones,
  Windflowers 65
Antirrhinum/
  Snapdragon 67
Aquilegia/Columbine 69
Arctotheca/African Daisy 69
Artemisia/Mugwort,
  Wormwood 70
Asclepias/Butterfly Weed,
  Milkweed 71
Aster/Aster 72
Astilbe/False Spiraea,
  Meadow Sweet 74
Begonia/Begonia 76
Calendula/Pot Marigold 78
Canna/Canna 79
Celosia/Cockscomb 80
Centaurea/Bachelor's
  Buttons, Cornflower 81
Chrysanthemum/
  Chrysanthemum 83
Cleome/Spider Flower 85
Coleus/Coleus 85
Convallaria/Lily-of-the-
  Valley 86
Cosmos/Cosmos 87
Crocus/Crocus 88
Dahlia/Dahlia 89
Delphinium/Delphinium 90
Dianthus/Cottage Pinks,
  Border Carnations 92
Dicentra/Bleeding Heart 93
Digitalis/Foxglove 94
Echinacea/Purple
  Coneflower 95
Gladiolus/Gladiolus 96
Gypsophila/Baby's
  Breath 97
Helianthus/Sunflower 98
Hemerocallis/Daylilies 99
Heuchera/Coralbells 100
Hosta/Funkia,
  Plantain Lily 101
Hyacinthus/Hyacinth 102
Iberis/Candytuft 103
Impatiens/Impatiens 104
Iris/Iris 105
Lathyrus/Sweet Pea 106
Lilium/Lily 107
Lobelia/Lobelia 108

Lobularia maritima/
  Sweet Alyssum 109
Lupinus/Lupine 110
Myosotis/Forget-Me-Not 111
Narcissus/Daffodil 112
Nicotiana/Flowering
  Tobacco 113
Paeonia/Peony 115
Papaver/Poppy 117
Pelargonium/Zonal
  Geranium 118
Penstemon/Penstemon 121
Petunia/Petunia 122
Phlox/Phlox 124
Rosa/Rose 125
Rudbeckia/Black-Eyed
  Susan 128
Sedum/Sedum 129
Senecio/Dusty Miller 130
Tagetes/Marigold 131
Tropaeolum/Nasturtium 133
Tulipa/Tulip 134
Verbena/Verbena 135
Veronica/Veronica 136
Viola/Pansy 137
Zinnia/Zinnia 137

CHAPTER 4

PREVENTION GLOSSARY 138

Means of Prevention 140
Natural Pesticides and
  Fungicides 142
Synthetic Pesticides and
  Fungicides 146
Beneficial Insects 150
Solarizing Soil 151

Source List 152
Plant Hardiness Zone Map 153
Index of Plants 154
General Index 156
Photo/Illustration Credits 160

A Walk in the Garden

Some years ago, an old-fashioned business management concept became popular in this country. Its acronym was MBWA, which stood for "management by walking around." The idea was that instead of managers hiding out in their offices, they should walk around the entire business on a regular basis to see firsthand how things were going, keeping their eyes and ears wide open while they were at it. Based as it was on such common sense, MBWA produced a lot of success for its practitioners.

Home gardeners who want to avoid problems from pests and diseases should consider a similar "management" approach.

The most important phrase in managing garden problems is "at the first sign of attack." For any garden problem, whether it's from animal or insect pests, or from one disease or another, there will be far less damage—and what damage there is will be far easier to control—if you catch it "at the first sign of attack." And there's no way of catching a problem in the early stages if the only view you ever have of your garden is from behind a window!

Garden management by walking around doesn't have to be work—in fact, it should be downright pleasant. During the growing season—from early spring through fall—get into the habit of touring your garden every day. Depending on your schedule, an early-morning, before-work walk through your garden, cup of coffee in hand, can start your day on a graceful note while keeping you informed on the health of your garden plants.

If an early-morning walk doesn't fit your schedule, how

about touring your garden in the evening, with a sundowner in hand instead of coffee? The point: Get out into your garden every day, keeping your eyes open for that all-important "first sign of attack."

Another cardinal rule in avoiding garden problems is that healthy plants in thriving condition are far likelier to stay that way than straggly, weak plants. As part of the big scheme of things, insects and diseases "know" to attack the least healthy plants first.

The gardener who wants to avoid problems should strive to keep each and every plant in his or her garden in thriving condition. And the best way to do that is to read chapter 1—Avoiding Problems. It includes a special essay called "A Balanced Approach" written by one of this country's most respected garden authorities, Rosalind Creasy; it is offered as food for thought for concerned gardeners everywhere. If you provide your plants with the right soil, give them the right amount of water and nutrients, choose them with their adaptability to your climate in mind, and

always favor disease-resistant varieties, you'll be surprised at how few problems ever plague your garden.

Gardeners know the entire subject of pest and disease control has become a controversial issue. While we at the National Home Gardening Club are here to help members garden better, we're not in the position to settle this particular controversy to every gardener's satisfaction.

But just as the "management by walking around" approach is based on common sense, we also believe there's a common-sense approach to pest and disease control. To this end, you'll find that throughout this book the various controls for each problem are listed in order of the most benign to the most extreme, in terms of toxicity and long-term effects on our environment. If your plants are in good shape to begin with, and if you catch a problem at the first sign of attack, the most benign controls work surprisingly well.

A garden may seem somewhat insignificant when viewed against the environment as a whole, but every home garden is like a square of fabric that makes up a larger patchwork quilt. The adage "think global, act local" is nowhere more pronounced than in each of our gardens. We are in fact stewards of this one small slice of the environment—a small piece of paradise, if you will. Treat it wisely and with care—using the ideas in this book—and the rewards will be great.

Good gardening!

A. Cort Sinnes

A. Cort Sinnes

◦ CHAPTER 1 ◦
AVOIDING PROBLEMS: THE BASICS

Talk to anyone who's gardened in the same location for a long time and they'll probably tell you that they don't have many problems from pests and diseases. What's their secret? When you take care of the same plot of land, season after season, a few simple truths gradually become clear: There's no substitute for good soil, and you have to provide what the plant needs in terms of water, nutrients and climate. The result? A healthy, thriving garden that's unattractive to pests and diseases. If you abide by the "rules" outlined in this chapter, you too will be pleasantly surprised at how few problems plague your garden.

SOIL PREPARATION—THE ALL-IMPORTANT FIRST STEP

Nothing, repeat nothing, is more important to the successful, healthy growth of plants than proper advance soil preparation. Skip this all-important first step and you're simply asking for trouble. Abide by it, and you've taken a huge step toward insuring a thriving, trouble-free garden.

Briefly stated, no matter what type of soil you find in your backyard—from the sandiest sand to the heaviest clay—a liberal addition of organic matter works miracles. The organic matter can be anything from homemade compost to well-rotted leafmold, fine fir bark or peat moss. Almost every area of the country lays claim to some indigenous, inexpensive organic material that is readily available in bulk quantities from nurseries and garden supply centers. Some communities even make compost available to local homeowners for free, the material having been made from the leaves gathered by municipal crews in the fall.

If you want to maintain a healthy soil, make abundant, yearly additions of an organic soil amendment to your garden beds, ideally either in the fall or spring.

The amount of organic matter to add should be equal to the depth that you intend to turn the soil. If you're preparing the soil to plant a lawn, whether it's from seed or sod, the minimum depth you should till is 6 inches; 8 or 12 inches is that much better. This may contradict some traditional advice, but experience has proven it very successful. If you intend to till the soil to a depth of 8 inches, add 8 inches of organic material on top of the soil before you till to incorporate it to the full depth. This takes some doing, but it helps develop an extensive, healthy root system, which results in a hardy, vigorous lawn, able to withstand droughts, diseases and pests.

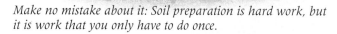

Make no mistake about it: Soil preparation is hard work, but it is work that you only have to do once.

Turning the soil relieves compaction, increases aeration and makes it easier for plant roots to get a maximum hold in the soil.

A wide variety of soil amendments are available at your local garden center or nursery. Check also to see if your community offers low-cost compost from leaves or other material.

Chicken Manure

Steer Manure

Vermiculite

Sand

Peat Moss

Compost

Loam

Gypsum

The same holds true for shrub borders, flower beds, areas intended for groundcovers and even vegetable gardens. Before planting, till groundcover areas to a depth of 8 to 12 inches; flower beds and vegetable gardens, to a depth of 6 to 8 inches.

Depending on what you are planting and the characteristics of your native soil, you may want to add fertilizer and lime as you incorporate the organic matter. Explain your situation to your local nursery or garden center to find out if such additions are necessary.

After tilling the organic matter into the soil, rake the area smooth and plant your plants. Build small dikes around individual plants (roughly the diameter of the root ball), and keep them well watered for the first few weeks after planting. In such superior soil, you'll be amazed at the growth they put on, even in the first year.

A Soil Test

If you are planning to put in a lawn, vegetable garden, perennial border, flower garden—any type of garden at all—or if you are having soil-related problems in an established garden, a soil test can solve many mysteries. Taking a test sample and having it analyzed are neither lengthy

nor difficult processes. The information contained in the report lets you be more accurate in improving the soil for specific plants. And making specific, needed improvements is far superior to the hit-and-miss method of adding fertilizers, lime or soil conditioners in unknown amounts.

Some state universities will test soil free of charge; others perform routine tests for a nominal fee. In the few states where universities do not provide this service, you should contact a private soil-testing laboratory; look in the yellow pages of your telephone book under "Laboratories, testing." If you do not find a listing, call your county agriculture extension agent and ask for a recommendation.

You should collect soil samples three to four months before you intend to plant your garden. This will give you ample time to get the test report back from the laboratory and make the necessary soil improvements before planting.

Soil pH is an important component for growing healthy plants. Check at your local nursery for a pH meter; test your soil and then adjust it accordingly.

Overly alkaline soil often causes plant foliage to turn yellow; one of the ways to acidify the soil is to add garden sulfur to the affected beds.

WATER

Over the years, a variety of sprinklers have come and gone. This "tractor" type sprinkler is a perennial favorite and intriguing to watch as it follows the path of the hose.

General advice on when and how to water a specific site is difficult because there are so many variables to be considered: soil type and slope, the plant's specific water requirements, weather conditions—including temperature, humidity, light intensity and wind—and whether the soil is covered with a mulch, all play a role in determining how much water your plants require.

All these factors are best known to you, the caretaker of your own garden, so the first word of advice should be to "know your garden"—the characteristics of the soil and plants, as well as your garden's location, combine to affect your watering practices. You will soon develop an art of watering that transcends the technical advice any book can offer. That said, the following information is a sound, general guideline for watering.

General Guidelines

The characteristics of your own soil are the single most important factor influencing your watering practices. If you've improved your soil to the point where it has the characteristics of "loam," more than half the watering battle is already won. Plants grown in a good loam soil are far more tolerant of a range of watering practices—whether it's too much or too little—than if they are grown in either a clay or sandy soil, both of which are notoriously difficult to water properly. This isn't to say that you can't learn to handle a clay or sandy soil successfully, but it's a challenge, involving much trial and error.

Loam, the ideal garden soil, admits nearly all the water that falls on it, holds a large quantity within the fine pores, allows any excess to drain away, and deters excessive evaporation by a layer of mulch.

With a clay soil, water enters slowly; overwatering causes flooding which, in turn, deprives plant roots of oxygen, causing the waterlogged plant to decline or die. Gardeners who manage clay soil learn to develop a rhythm of what is basically "too much and too little": Alternate periods of wetting and partial drying of the soil. The drying periods allow air to enter the soil.

Sandy soils provide fast drainage and excellent aeration,

Drip irrigation has proven to be a real boon to home gardeners, saving water and delivering it in optimum amounts. Many types of systems are available; shown here is one which "oozes" water.

Loam—that ideal garden soil—admits nearly all the water that falls on it, hangs on to the water long enough for roots to get their fill, then drains well to allow oxygen to return to the spaces between the soil particles.

Some drip irrigation systems can be almost completely camouflaged with a layer of soil or mulch, allowing only the emitter to show through.

but fail in the water-holding department. Generally speaking, the coarser the particles that make up a soil, the less water the soil will hold. Sandy soils (which have the coarsest particles of all) hold only about $1/4$ inch of water per foot of depth. Sandy loams commonly hold about $3/4$ inch of water per foot; fine sandy loams, about $1 1/4$ inches; and silt loams, clay loams, and clays, about $2 1/2$ to 3 inches. Although these are rough figures, they clearly show that different soil types demand different watering schedules.

Adding organic matter to any of the soil types mentioned above will work to equalize their water requirements: Large amounts of organic matter will increase the water-holding capacity of sandy soils, and will "open" heavier silt loams and clay soils, allowing more air and water to enter.

How Much and When?

Here are a couple of time-honored rules to follow when it comes to watering.

The first rule concerns the amount of water to apply at any one time, and it is as simple as it is important: Fill the root zone with water and then allow the soil to dry out somewhat before you water again.

If you water too thoroughly and too frequently, there's a good chance you'll cut off the supply of air in the soil by filling all of the air spaces with water. Root growth will stop, and the longer the air is cut off, the greater the root damage. Damaged roots are prime targets for rot-causing microorganisms, usually resulting in the plant's death from root rot.

On the other hand, if you water too lightly and too frequently, water never has a chance to move very far into the soil. In order to thrive, all plants need moisture, nutrients and air. The soil surrounding a plant's roots may be nutrient-rich and contain plenty of air, but without moisture, roots will simply not grow there. The result of repeated shallow watering is shallow-rooted plants. If you miss a couple of waterings, a shallow-rooted plant does not have the ability to tap reserves of moisture deeper in the soil. Consequently, the plant cannot survive even brief periods of drought or high temperatures.

To repeat the first rule of watering: When you water, water well and then learn how long it takes for your particular soil to dry out slightly between waterings. How can you tell if you're watering thoroughly? The best way is to take a look underground a couple of hours after you've watered. Use a shovel or a trowel to get past the top 3 or 4 inches of soil. You'll be able to tell by the color and texture of the soil how far the water has penetrated into the soil (moist soil will be darker and softer than dry soil). If the soil isn't moist past the top 4 inches, you're not watering enough.

General rule number two concerns the often asked question: "When is the best time to water?" There are plenty of local prejudices and differing schools of thought on this subject, but com-

Hand watering may be the least practical—but most enjoyable—of all the means of irrigation available to home gardeners.

mon sense may be the best advice of all. You can reduce plant diseases and lose less water to evaporation by watering in the early morning. The reasoning behind this is clear: Leaves (including blades of grass) that stay damp through the night invite attack by disease-causing organisms. By watering in the morning hours, you give plants a chance to dry off before nightfall, thus eliminating the conditions in which diseases thrive.

In-ground sprinkler systems can be completely automated, allowing gardeners to leave home on a summer vacation without worrying about whether or not their plants will survive.

FERTILIZERS

Garden soils are a combination of organic and mineral components, and two processes make the nutrients available for use by plants: 1) living soil organisms—often referred to as beneficial bacteria—break down and release the nutrients found in the organic matter; and 2) the natural process of degradation—the effects of sun, wind, rain, and freezing and thawing—make the mineral elements available.

Knowing this, the next logical question is: Why, if there are nutrients already in the soil, is it necessary to add more in the form of fertilizer? The answer is simple: Although the amount of nutrients in most soils is relatively high in comparison to a plant's requirements, many nutrients are either in a form plants cannot use, or are

Local sources of composted poultry or horse manure are usually quite reasonable in price; any composted manure will improve the quality of the soil and have moderate fertilizer value, as well.

not supplied fast enough to produce satisfactory plant growth. Farmers and gardeners alike turn to fertilizers to make up for this deficiency. Thus, fertilizers play a considerable part in keeping plants in thriving condition—and plants in thriving condition are the least likely to be bothered by pests and diseases.

All fertilizers, whether natural,

organic or synthesized, contain some or all of the nutrient elements essential for plant growth. In whatever amounts they are present, these elements are what make a fertilizer a fertilizer.

The truth of the matter is that most plants are perfectly happy with a general purpose, balanced fertilizer; only a few, such as azaleas and rhododendrons, require specialized formulations.

Organic gardeners prefer organic fertilizers, which contribute to the general health of the soil, as opposed to chemical fertilizers which simply feed the plants.

THE SIXTEEN ESSENTIAL NUTRIENTS

The first three elements listed below—carbon, hydrogen and oxygen—are derived primarily from the atmosphere and water. The other elements are absorbed by plant roots from the surrounding soil. These 13 elements are of primary importance to farmers and gardeners around the world. They are most often supplied by soil, fertilizer or both.

Primary Elements:	Macronutrients:	Secondary Nutrients:	Micronutrients:	Iron (Fe)
Carbon (C)	Nitrogen (N)	Calcium (Ca)	Boron (B)	Manganese (Mn)
Hydrogen (H)	Phosphorus (P)	Magnesium (Mg)	Chlorine (Cl)	Molybdenum (Mo)
Oxygen (O)	Potassium (K)	Sulfur (S)	Copper (Cu)	Zinc (Zn)

The Essential Plant Nutrients

There are currently more than 100 known chemical elements. Of these, there are only 16 that have definitely been determined to be essential for plant growth, and recent research suggests there might be one more. These elements are considered essential because without any one of them, plant growth will not occur, even if the other elements are present in their required amounts.

The box above shows a list of the 16 elements now known to be essential for plant growth. Other elements—cobalt and nickel—are now thought to be essential for specific groups of plants.

When there's too little nitrogen in the soil, plants will be slow growing or stunted with pale leaves, rather than the robust green foliage you want.

Basic Fertilizer Practices

The average home gardener grows perhaps 30 to 40 different types of plants and trees. Out of that total number, only a few really need any "personalized" feeding program. The rest will grow very satisfactorily with a minimum of attention from the gardener if—and this is a big "if"—the basic requirements for a plant to grow have been satisfied from the beginning, including a soil amended with plenty of organic matter, regular, deep watering, and matching the right plant with the right location.

Although its value as a fertilizer is low, compost adds to the overall health of your soil and is absolutely one of the best amendments you can add.

When it comes time to fertilize, home gardeners may begin to doubt just how simple the process really is—the number of different forms and formulations of today's fertilizer products can be bewildering. And although you wouldn't guess it, the amount of information any gardener needs to know concerning commercially available fertilizers is relatively limited and basic. All fertilizer products have a great deal in common.

The first step is to understand the label. All commercial fertilizers are labeled with the percentages they contain of nitrogen, phosphorus and potassium—the macronutrients. There are many formulations—24-4-8, 5-10-10, 12-6-6, 16-16-16 and so on—but the listings are always in the same order with nitrogen first, followed by phosphorus, and potassium last—note the alphabetical order. Even fertilizers that are not complete, that is, those containing only one or two of the macronutrients, are still labeled the same: 0-10-10, 0-20-0, 21-0-0, 0-0-60, for example.

One general rule holds true for all fertilizers: The percentage of nitrogen in the formula dictates the amount of fertilizer to be applied. Why? Too much nitrogen can burn, or even kill, a plant. As is the case with any commercially available garden product, whether it's an insecticide, fungicide or fertilizer, you

Simple and effective: Mix a liquid fertilizer with water in an old-fashioned watering can and deliver it to just those plants that need feeding.

must read and follow all label directions to the letter.

Fertilizer Forms

Fertilizers also come in many different forms such as dry, liquid, slow-release, organic, pelleted and soluble. The reason for the great variety of formulations and forms has a lot to do with the personal habits of gardeners. Different liquid, dry, or slow-release fertilizers may all have the same percentages of nitrogen, phosphorus and potassium, and even the same micronutrients. But one gardener will prefer to add a dry fertilizer to a soil mixture, while another gardener wants to mix the liquid form in a hose sprayer and feed the entire

yard at once, while yet another gardener who specializes in hanging baskets, may want to fertilize as few times as possible and use a pelleted, slow-release form.

The number of different formulations available is the result of research into the specific needs of specific plants. While there are a great many plants

Pelleted, slow-release fertilizers are excellent for plants in containers. Feeding once a month is about right, but some slow-release fertilizers need only yearly applications.

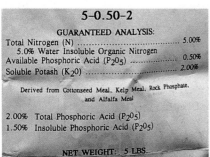

The three numbers on every bag of fertilizer denote the percentage of nitrogen, phosphorus and potassium (N, P, K) present in that particular formulation. As you can see, the fertilizer on the left has 5% nitrogen, .5% phosphorus, and 2% potassium, while the one on the right is "balanced", with 10% of each nutrient.

Rhododendrons—one of the aristocrats of all garden plants—require an acidic soil to reach their peak perfection.

Related to the rhododendron (pictured above), azaleas also require an acidic soil, that can be achieved using a fertilizer that is acidic in reaction. Or add acidifying soil amendments like pine needles or peat moss.

"customized" fertilizer. The most common flowering plants requiring a specialized fertilizer are collectively known as the "acid-lovers," which include azaleas, rhododendrons, camellias, daphne and gardenias. For the best results, feed these special plants with a fertilizer that is acidic in reaction (which will be stated on the label); one form is not necessarily better than another, so use the one that best suits your gardening habits.

Fertilizing Flowers

Different groups of garden plants have different fertilizer needs. Vegetable plants, for example, have high fertilizer needs while evergreen shrubs and trees have low nutrient needs. Flower gardens fall somewhere in between. Annual flowers have a moderate need for fertilizer; perennial flowers have a medium to low need. In practice, annual flowers will need an application of fertilizer every four to six weeks during the growing season; annual flowers grown in containers require a once-a-month feeding. Perennial flowers will get by with an early spring feeding and

Perennial flowers, such as these coneflowers, require less fertilizer than annuals; they will get by with a feeding in early spring and one additional application after they flower.

one additional application of fertilizer after they flower. Remember, the goal is to keep the plant healthy and thriving—a state where they are able to resist attacks by insects and diseases. Conversely, a plant that is weak and barely growing is a prime target for every pest and disease that comes along.

that do not have such specific needs, there are many that will give the gardener superior results only when the plants are given special care, including a

To maintain peak performance, annual flowers (such as these snapdragons) require feeding with a complete fertilizer once every four to six weeks throughout the growing season.

Flowering shrubs and evergreens have a lower need for fertilizer than either annuals or perennials: One spring feeding each year is ample.

THE RIGHT PLANT IN THE RIGHT PLACE

Gardeners save themselves a lot of heartache by simply matching the right plants to a particular location. This full-sun location is just the thing for zinnias and marigolds—both of which will take as much sun and warmth as you can give them.

When it's time to select plants for your garden, most people start with a list of their favorite plants. If you're looking for the least amount of upkeep—and the fewest problems from pests and diseases—this is not the way to go about planting your garden.

Every geographic and climatic region of the country has plants well suited to its particular conditions. These are grasses, annuals, perennials, shrubs, vines and trees that display an admirable willingness to grow. They may not be the most unusual plants; in fact, most of them will be quite common. But a common plant that is in thriving condition is far more attractive and easy to maintain than a rare plant that only limps along.

In addition to choosing plants appropriate to your region, select individual plants well suited to the exact location you intend to plant them. When you go to the nursery or garden center, know the exposure of each of your planting sites—does a particular site receive only morning sun, hot afternoon sun from 2 o'clock on, or dappled sunlight under a large deciduous tree? Explain the growing conditions to the salesperson, describe how big the area is, and then request to see appropriate plants for each specific location in your yard. When choosing any plant—but especially trees or shrubs—select only those plants that will physically fit, when mature, into the allotted space. This will all but eliminate the need to prune, and your plant will be allowed to achieve its natural form rather than some abstract geometric shape resulting from repeated trimming.

If the plant selection process sounds like it takes a fair amount of research and effort, it does. But you don't have to be the one to go through the effort or

When that first really warm spring day arrives, good gardeners everywhere flock to their local nursery to see what's available. Just remember not to get too excited purchasing plants that aren't suited to your garden's conditions—no matter now pretty they are!

Finding the right exposure is one of the most important aspects of matching plants with a site. Here a bed with light shade and dappled sun creates the perfect environment for ferns, ivies and other shade-loving plants.

do the research. Most reputable nurseries will provide you with a custom planting plan, usually free of charge, if you agree to purchase the plants from their nursery. In most cases, this is a fair trade-off. Just let them know that you want plants with marked willingness to grow in your location, and then leave the selection process in their capable hands.

Once the plants have been selected, how you plant them will have a significant effect on their ultimate performance. "Soil preparation" has an unglamorous ring to it, but when done correctly, it can help produce some very glamorous results (see "Soil Preparation—The All-Important First Step" on pages 10-11).

As you're improving the soil, it may seem to be nothing more than a lot of hard work. But no other step will pay off more handsomely in the long run. A plant that has to struggle to survive because of difficult soil conditions will grow slowly, lack vigor, be subject to attack from pests and diseases, and never quite meet your expectations. One of the most overlooked

facts in gardening is that a healthy, vigorous plant will need next to no attention from the gardener, while a weak plant will need more or less constant assistance in the form of sprays and assorted tonics.

Most plants grown by commercial nurseries include a label containing information as to what kind of environment that particular plant prefers; read the label and follow the recommendations.

Good soil preparation, a little water, a little fertilizer and the right plant for the right place—it's a winning combination that produces beautiful, thriving plants.

RESISTANT VARIETIES

Continued efforts by plant breeders have made great strides in producing plants resistant to diseases. With the onset of genetic engineering, home gardeners will undoubtedly see more disease- and even pest-resistant plants in the future. If you've had trouble with diseases on a particular plant in the past, by all means check to see if there is a disease-resistant variety available.

If you are set on planting a specific plant for which there are no disease-resistant varieties, the old adage "an ounce of prevention is worth a pound of cure" rings true. Once a disease strikes a plant, further damage can be prevented with the application of a fungicide, but the present damage cannot be eradicated. If you know a particular plant is susceptible to attack from disease, go on the offensive before the disease appears to prevent it from becoming a problem. This means applying a fungicide as a preventative measure before the first symptoms appear.

Most of the old-fashioned varieties of asters are known for their susceptibility to mildew. This beauty, Aster x frikartii *'Wood's Pink', is an exception, being extremely mildew-resistant. Specifically search for disease-resistant varieties like this.*

DISEASE-RESISTANT VARIETIES:

Rust-resistant snapdragons: 'Deluxe', 'Double Sweetheart' and 'Royal Carpet'.

Rust-resistant roses: 'Cécile Brunner', 'Europeana', 'Fragrant Cloud', 'Garden Pat', 'Iceberg', 'Miss All-American Beauty', 'Sexy Rexy', 'Souvenir de la Malmaison' and 'Tropicana'.

'Cecile Brunner', an old-fashioned favorite, is a rust-resistant variety of rose.

Black spot-resistant roses: 'Bonica', 'Carefree Beauty', 'Dr. W. van Fleet', 'Flower Carpet', 'Iceberg', 'Olympiad', 'Mrs. B.R. Grant' and 'Queen Elizabeth'.

Generally disease-resistant roses: 'Abraham Darby', 'Ballerina', 'Betty Prior', 'Buff Beauty', 'Duchesse de Brabant', 'Enchantress', 'Lady Bank's Rose', 'Lamarque', 'Margo Koster', 'Marie van Houtte', 'Mister Lincoln', 'Nearly Wild', 'New Dawn', 'Old Blush', 'Perle D'or', 'Simplicity', 'The Fairy', 'Zéphirine Drouhin'.

Topping the list of many people's favorite roses is the prolific 'Iceberg', a real winner and black spot-resistant to boot!

Mildew-resistant asters: *Aster* x *frikartii*, 'Wood's Pink'.

Borer-resistant iris: Siberian iris (*Iris sibirica*) and its many named cultivars.

Iris sibirica 'Ruffled Velvet' is not only a show-stopper, it is also borer-resistant.

Mildew-resistant phlox: 'David', 'Eva Cullum', 'Franz Schubert', 'Katherine', 'Pax', 'Sandra', *Phlox carolina* and *P. divaricata*.

Mildew-resistant zinnias: *Zinnia angustifolia*.

Mildew-resistant crepe myrtles: 'Acoma', 'Biloxi', 'Hopi', 'Lipan', 'Miami', 'Natchez', 'Sioux', 'Yuma', and 'Zuni'.

Lilies resistant to lily mosaic: *Lilium amabile, L. brownii, L. davidii, L. hansonii, L. henryii, L. martagon, L. monadelphum, L. pardalinum, L. pumilum, L. regale*.

Many phlox varieties are plagued with mildew. The good-looking 'Wild Sweet William' blooms prolifically and is mildew-resistant.

Gardeners embrace roses like 'Ballerina'—it's not only beautiful, but very easy to grow and rarely bothered by any disease.

Mildew can be a real problem with zinnias, especially in regions with humid summers. The small-flowered Zinnia angustifolia is amazingly mildew-resistant.

ANIMALS—THE BIG PESTS

No question about it—it's very exciting to see wildlife up close, but if you have to share a garden with them, the excitement can quickly turn to frustration.

Besides insects and diseases, home gardeners are often prey to large, four-footed pests such as deer, moles, gophers, rabbits, voles and field mice. If your garden has ever been beset by any of these creatures, you know just how frustrating controlling them can be. If you live in an area populated by deer, you'll no doubt be able to relate to the following essay (through page 27) by Rosalind Creasy, one of this country's leading garden authorities.

Deer Dilemma

One very foggy morning 20 years ago, my husband and I looked out the kitchen window. There on the front lawn, a mere 10 feet away, was a magnificent buck. What a thrill, we thought—a genuine wild animal right here in our cheek-to-jowl suburban neighborhood! It's true that an occasional deer sighting is exciting. But when a family of deer is devouring your every tulip, or you find a buck has snapped a young apple tree midtrunk, it's heartbreaking.

I was once a wide-eyed Bambi lover, but now I've found murder in my heart for these destructive pests. A hundred years ago, Americans viewed deer as a source of meat for the winter. Today, as a nation of urbanites, many view hunting with suspicion. In the meantime, we have exterminated the deer's natural predators, landscaped our yard with millions of their favorite foods, and enacted ordinances to protect them. This has resulted in a drastic overpopulation, and left

Just yesterday these sunflowers were in their full summer glory; an overnight feeding by deer reduced them to a mere shadow of their former selves.

many homeowners watching their landscaping nipped to ankle height. In addition, countless deer die a slow death by disease or starvation—in my opinion, a far more cruel way to die than from a predator's attack or hunter's bullet. Ecologists are also alarmed at how deer over-browsing seriously endangers native plant communities already weakened by humans. In fact, in many botanical circles, deer are considered "jaws with fur."

After years of managing my clients' deer problems as a landscape designer, I've amassed an array of deterrents and barriers to control the damage done by deer. The only completely effective solution I've found is deer fencing, particularly where gardens are surrounded by deer and filled with such irresistible deer yummies as roses, azaleas, vegetables, tulips and fruit trees.

For gardeners who are troubled by only an occasional deer, alternatives to fencing are to plant deer-resistant plants, create a yard with large, wide-open expanses of lawn, or plant a mass of junipers and other forgiving plants. I've also found that bird netting can help foil these four-footed foragers.

Young trees, especially, need protection from deer, even during the winter months. Here sturdy wire cages protect newly planted Japanese cut-leaf maples.

Fencing

As fencing is the most effective way to control deer damage, let's begin by looking at how deer behave and what makes an effective fence.

Deer are prodigious jumpers—it's common for them to jump or leap up to 8 feet. However, given a choice, a deer would rather go under or through a fence than over it. That means the most effective deer fences are at least 8 feet tall and are constructed flush to the ground. Fawns can squeeze under a barrier that has only 6 inches of clearance. Also, be on the lookout for potential entry holes under the fence made by raccoons and skunks.

If for some reason a tall fence is not suitable for your garden site, there are other options.

Deer are cautious, and they avoid jumping into areas that they can't see. That means you can get by with a shorter fence if you plant a line of taller, bushy, solid evergreens alongside of it. You can also use two parallel 4- or 5-foot-tall fences and then plant shrubs between them.

Even if they don't feed on your plants, bucks rubbing their antlers against the bark of trees can rub them raw, often resulting in a dead tree.

Crows are among the most agressive of all birds, causing damage not only to gardens, but creating general havoc with other birds.

For such timid creatures, deer are amazingly bold when it comes to entering your garden and helping themselves to your plants.

Electric fences work well and are much less expensive than wooden or chain-link barriers, provided there aren't young children or pets nearby that might accidentally touch the fence. Electric fences are fairly short (4 feet is a good height) and are best constructed with three strings of 14-gauge wire—one strung across the top, one midway to the ground, and one along the bottom, 18 inches off the ground. The fences are attached to a power supply and produce a small shock when touched. The shock startles, but no permanent harm is done. Smaller (even portable) electric fences can be effective for a small vegetable garden. Deer do not try to jump over these fences but instead put their head or body

Cute as can be, racoons can be a problem in home gardens; keep garbage cans tightly covered and don't feed pets outdoors.

Do Fence Me In

The minimum height for an effective deer fence is 8 feet. The fence should be flush against the ground, as deer can squeeze through even the smallest space.

Where 8-foot-tall fences aren't practical, an effective alternative is a 4- to 5-foot-tall fence with closely-planted evergreens lining one side. The goal is to create a visual barrier, because deer won't jump into a spot they can't see.

A variation is to construct two 4- to 5-foot-tall parallel fences separated by a row of evergreens. Although this may sound a bit extreme, it actually creates a very effective barrier.

A less expensive—and less conspicuous—solution where kids and pets are not a concern is to use electric fencing. This fence is best constructed using three lines of wire, with the bottom wire 18 inches above the ground. Interestingly, deer don't try to jump these fences, seeking instead to climb between the wires. When they do, the fences generate a mild but effective shock that warns the animals away from further attempts.

Look closely and you'll see three strands of electrified wire above this quaint picket fence—the result? Good looks and good protection from deer.

through, get a shock, and learn to avoid the area. Most farm supply stores have materials and information on installing electric fences. By the way: All fences are enhanced by having a resident snarling dog around.

Other Deer Repellents

Sometimes it's not appropriate or practical to construct a fence. In that case, other mechanical barriers, repellents, and/or plants that deer find unpalatable are required. I'm presently involved in a landscaping project with these parameters, and it serves as an opportunity to reexamine the range of control techniques now available.

My clients in Los Altos Hills, California, have a home that is situated on two acres. Their backyard is well fenced, but the front yard slopes up to the street, unprotected. It wasn't practical to put a high fence across the driveway in front, and visiting grandchildren precluded the use of an electric fence. Two does and their offspring also call this lovely area "home."

Although no recommendation of deer-proof plants is infallible, they do seem to avoid bearded iris in most locations.

Although grape hyacinths are listed as "deer-proof" in many sources, in reality deer avoid it in some regions and gobble it up in others.

What squirrels eat depends largely on how hungry they are: During the summer when there's plenty to eat, they'll leave a lot of plants alone; during the winter, however, they may eat anything in sight.

The aesthetic goal of the landscape design was to plant the hillside with numerous drought-tolerant perennials and groundcovers that provide lots of color. The colors chosen were a dramatic combination of apricot, burgundy and lavender. I planned to incorporate many plants with burgundy foliage, and I also included a small culinary herb garden.

My first step was to consult the deer-resistant list in *The Sunset Western Garden Book*, the bible of gardeners in the western states. To this list of possible plants, I added the names of plants I had used successfully in other deer ares. We planned to plant items that the deer tended to ignore, namely redwoods (*Sequoia sempervirens*), star jasmine (*Trachelospermum jasminoides*), lily-of-the-Nile (*Agapanthus* spp.), bearded iris, daffodils and grape hyacinths. To get a list of "deerproof" plants for your area, contact your local university cooperative extension service. The number is located under the county or state listing in the phone book. In addition, Cornell University has a plant list that is applicable to much of the Northeast. You can order this by contacting them at (607) 255-2080.

As we began the landscape installation, I was well aware that every deer-resistant plant list contains caveats about not being foolproof. But it was clear that these deer had never even read the list—over half the plants listed were munched! Fortunately, we had covered many plants (those I thought might be the most delectable) with black plastic bird netting. Thus protected, these plants were fine. However, the uncovered Japanese anemones, coralbells (*Heuchera sanguinea*), rockroses (*Cistus* spp.), potato vine (*Solanum jasminoides*), hop bush (*Dodonaea viscosa*), cape plumbago (*Plumbago auriculata*), yarrow (*Achillea* spp.), Serbian bellflower (*Campanula poscharskyana*), *Centranthus ruber*, sea lavender (*Limonium*), sedum 'Autumn Joy', yellow lantana

Floating row covers offer some protection from rabbits, but the only real remedy is fencing at least 2 feet tall. If you use a pliable wire, like chicken wire, bury the bottom edge 6 inches deep to keep rabbits from pushing up openings.

(*Lantana camara*), penstemons, gaura (*Gaura lindheimeri*), butterfly bush (*Buddleia davidii*), dwarf lion's tail (*Leonotis leonurus*), and even the new plants of star jasmine were all chewed, most to the ground. The deer seemed especially partial to the plants with burgundy foliage.

Within a week after planting, we sprayed the most common commercial repellent, Hinder, on the plants we thought were most at risk. For a few weeks the deer moved on to the old agapanthus we had divided and to the old planting of star jasmine. In the meantime, I attended a Garden Writers Association of America convention and was bombarded with samples of deer repellents by many different purveyors.

Back home, two weeks later, the Hinder seemed to have worn off, and the deer were on a rampage again. For the most damaged plants, we purchased a dozen packages of bird netting and covered as many as we could. Then we decided to test several of the various commercially available deer repellents in separate areas of the garden.

We tested a sack of Bye-Deer, which is made from soaps and herbs and is designed to be hung in the plant; Deer-Off, a spray of putrid eggs and chile peppers; Mole-Med, a castor oil-based liquid designed to repel moles and also said to deter deer; and small, wicked bottles of predator urine—coyote, to be specific—to scare them off.

This was what we found:

1. **The Bye-Deer** seemed to protect the plant it was attached to, but with hundreds of plants on the property, this wasn't a practical solution.

2. **The Deer-Off** worked, as did the Hinder, but again, only for a few weeks. And as we were trying to protect plants in over a half acre of garden, it was really tedious to haul watering cans or hoses around to spray each plant.

3. **The Mole-Med** had no measurable impact.

4. **As for the coyote urine**, the deer actually seemed more active in the area where it was placed—we found footprints all over the hill. Maybe it was a coincidence, but we had placed one of the urine dispensers near the new terra-cotta birdbath, and the bath was knocked over and broken. Maybe the deer were spooked by the scent, but unfortunately, it didn't frighten them enough to make them move to a new territory.

Nurseries and garden centers offer a wide variety of deer and other animal deterrents, all of which, unfortunately, seem to work for some situations and not in others.

A relatively recent introduction, floating row covers protect plants from a wide variety of pests, including birds and rabbits.

Results for the Long Run

It's now been nearly a year since we first began this garden. We've installed a new birdbath, and this time it's anchored in cement and the top is glued to the base. So far, so good.

One of the does has now had triplets! All that great food, no doubt. There are lots of foot paths through the plantings as well as some trampling. However, the bulk of the plants are okay. Recovering under the bird netting are the penstemons, agapanthus, rockroses, yarrows, gaura and limonium. Still untouched are the tall burgundy pennisetum grasses, shore junipers (*Juniperus conferta*), asparagus ferns, bearded irises, apricot foxgloves (*Digitalis purpurea* 'Apricot'), Japanese maple, Mexican sages (*Salvia leucantha*), narcissus, lavender lantanas, euryops daisies (*Euryops pectinatus*), apricot oleanders (*Nerium oleander* 'Mrs. Roeding'), the Spanish and English lavenders (*Lavandula stoechas* and *L. angustifolia*), and the little herb garden with sage, oregano, rosemary, fennel, and common thyme with woolly thyme

It's always a toss-up with birds—between the damage some do to the garden, the pest control they may assist with, and the beauty they bring both in sight and sound.

(*Thymus pseudolanuginosus*), between the steppingstones.

We will leave the bird netting over the large plantings and hope that as the plants mature they will become more fibrous and less tasty. If not, at least they won't get uprooted as easily. Come summer we will replant the successful beds of ageratum and fibrous begonias near the house, because the deer left those alone. We'll also move the Japanese anemones, surviving coralbells and ivy geraniums to the back garden and replace them with junipers.

What remains is still a beautiful, if somewhat stressed, hillside garden. There are lots of new birds visiting the birdbath, and the hummingbirds enjoy the sages and penstemon flowers sticking up out of the netting. And we've all gotten used to the rather unobtrusive bird netting and are resigned to the fact that we won't be able to have all the types of plants we wanted.

What will the future bring besides more deer? Probably a few more heartbreaks. I'm sure we will lose a few more types of plants and suffer more trampling. It will be interesting to see how this little struggle between man and beast will play itself out over the years. It's a bit of a microcosm of a growing American phenomenon—wildlife and people finding ways to coexist.

Wicket-like hoops keep netting off plants below, protecting them from birds, rabbits and all insect pests.

Plastic netting or wire mesh seems to be the only way to deter squirrels completely; sprinkling around the plants with ground cayenne works during summer when squirrels have plenty to eat and aren't as determined as they are in winter.

An opening in the soil like this is a telltale sign of a woodchuck.

Gophers and Moles

Gophers and moles present a real problem to gardeners in many areas of the country.

How can you tell whether it's a gopher or mole causing the damage? A gopher eats roots, including bulbs, tubers and roots of trees, vines and shrubs; occasionally (and most shocking of all to the gardener) whole plants will disappear down their holes! Gophers tunnel from 6 to 12 inches under the soil and push the excavated dirt out to the surface, leaving small mounds of fine-particle earth. The mounds are not completely symmetrical.

The mole is considered insectivorous, eating larvae and worms, and occasionally tulip bulbs. The mole burrows so close to the soil's surface that you can plainly see his route. In the tunnel-making process, moles break off tender root systems, snap stems and uproot seedlings. Molehills are symmetrical, and look like small volcanoes. Unlike the gopher's pulverized soil, the

soil that makes up a molehill is in small, compact plugs.

Potential Cures

Down through gardening history have come many tried-and-not-so-true instructions for the eradication of these animals. For instance, there are those who have tried putting a garden hose into one of the runways in an attempt to flood them out; this is of dubious value at best, and at worst, an incredible waste of water. Others have tried attaching a garden hose to the tail pipe of an operating car, trying to gas the devils out with carbon monoxide—which is not only dangerous (and definitely not recommended), but a classic case of the cure being more trouble than the ailment. There are a number of commercially available traps, some of which claim high success rates (ask at your local nursery and follow the manufacturer's directions carefully).

Commercially poisoned grains are occasionally effective. And there are gas bombs that you light and stick into the hole. Or you may plant rows of a so-called "gopher plant" (*Euphorbia lathyris*) around the perimeter of your garden or planting bed. The roots and stems of the gopher plant contain a caustic poison that may, or may not (depending on who you talk to), repel furry subterranean invaders. Finally, there is the organized and studied placement of

wooden windmills called "Klippety-Klops" that send vibrations into the soil and reportedly scare moles and gophers away.

All these measures would begin to take on a comical quality if the damage done by gophers and moles wasn't so infuriating to gardeners, particularly when the creatures seem to outsmart the most diligent efforts to get rid of them.

Last Straw Controls

"Last straw" controls include two of the more direct and unquestionably effective methods.

One is to wait silently for hours over a new tunnel or hill for the creature to stick its unsuspecting head out, then whack it with a shovel or let go with a blast from a shotgun. Local ordinances rarely allow the use of a gun within city limits, but more than one country gopher has met his maker this way.

More practically, there seems to be only one surefire, albeit limited, method to control gophers and moles—and it falls into the "preventive measures" category. If you decide to build raised

If you were to make a list of the most frustrating garden pests, gophers and moles would certainly be near the top, seemingly immune to almost every deterrent.

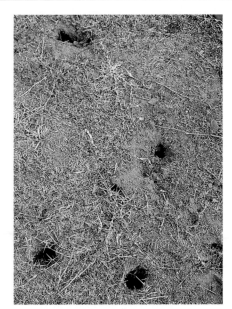

Any number of rodents can wreak havoc in a home garden, dotting the landscape with tunnels and holes. Unfortunately, burrowing rodents are notoriously difficult to control.

More than a few gardeners have resorted to the last line of defense against gophers and moles—raised beds lined with wire mesh—extreme, but effective.

beds (garden beds surrounded by landscape timbers, or the like, and filled with excellent topsoil) you can avoid all gopher and mole attacks in this defined area by lining the bed with 1/2-inch mesh wire before you fill it with soil. This is a particularly good idea for protecting expensive spring-flowering bulbs. For individual plants, shrubs and prized specimens, you can avoid damage using the same technique: Line the planting hole with 1/2-inch mesh wire.

Field Mice and Voles

These varmints are less of a problem in most gardens. When present, they may be as hard to eradicate as gophers and moles—in whose abandoned tunnels they often live—but their damage is easier to prevent. Instead of attacking plants underground, voles and field mice (and occasionally rabbits and porcupines) attack the aboveground portion of plants. They often "girdle" the base of trees and shrubs—gnaw the bark from around them. If enough of

the bark is removed, the tree will die with the first surge of spring growth. Protect the lower trunk, particularly in winter when attacks are common, with a cylinder of hardware cloth from the base of the trunk, up

24 inches or more. Check occasionally to be sure it doesn't become too tight as the tree grows.

Rat and mouse poison pellets work (be careful if you have pets) as do old-fashioned "indoor" mouse traps too.

The classic "Havaheart" trap continues to live up to its reputation as an effective and humane way of trapping furry pests.

A BALANCED APPROACH

By Rosalind Creasy

"Go gently on the earth," says Rosalind Creasy in this section created especially for this book. Her message? A balanced and organic approach will make your garden a healthier and more environmentally-friendly place. The principles already outlined in this chapter, along with the ideas on the next few pages, can go a long way toward reducing or even eliminating the need for chemicals. Soil, water, fertilizer, plant selection and placement, encouraging beneficial insects … they all add up to an environment "in sync" with itself and able to take care of many problems before they start. Sure, you still might need to break out a chemical or two occasionally, and you'll even read about them in this book as potential solutions *if all else fails*. But a balanced approach will reduce that need while increasing your gardening success and enjoyment.

Honeybees are among the most important insects in any garden—and also one of the most susceptible to the harmful effects of insecticides.

Over the past 30 years, I've evolved into what most people would call a fanatical gardener. Every inch of my Los Altos, California, yard is planted with some form of flower, vegetable or tree, and I change most of the planting plan twice a year. I get both pleasure and my livelihood from my garden, using it as a source for my photography and writing, and as a test plot for my business as a landscape designer. My entire professional life somehow grows out of this patch of ground, and I work on it constantly.

That said, you might be surprised to find that I am not outraged when I find aphids sucking happily on my ivy. I don't feel alarmed when I see larvae and caterpillars munching their way through a few of my flowers. I almost never spray my garden for insects or disease, even with so-called natural products such as pyrethrums, rotenone or nicotine. My garden is still beautiful, filled with healthy plants that fight off disease, and it's crawling with insects, both beneficial ones and pests. The secret? My garden is in balance.

As I've learned more about gardening, I've changed my approach to pests. When I began, I used chemicals to control them. By the early 1970s I had become heavily involved in environmental issues, and using heavy-duty chemicals in the garden ran counter to all I was learning. In response, I started to use pesticides that were "natural" rather than man-made.

Today, I've moved beyond even that. These days I want my garden to be as close to a natural ecosystem as I can manage—a garden where the inhabitants work together to solve their own problems. I am an organic gardener, and then some. My ideal is not to interfere at all with the natural system. Realistically, I'll never reach that. Instead, when I make choices about how I will tend my garden, I base my decision on how much damage any particular act causes to my ecosystem. I've also discovered that I generally don't need any

Author and natural gardener extraordinaire, Rosalind Creasy in her home garden.

It may be a standard-sized suburban lot, but Ros Creasy's exhuberant approach to gardening makes it anything but commonplace.

pesticides—natural or man-made—when my garden is brimming with beneficial birds and insects that control the insect pests that would harm my plants.

I've also come to understand that the occasional gnawed leaf or slightly imperfect fruit is the modest price I pay for gardening gently on the earth.

The Holistic Garden

My first experience with a garden whose insect world was out of balance came in 1967. We had just purchased our present house, and the previous owner gave me the card of a monthly pesticide spraying service she had been using. I hesitated at first, but she assured me that the service was safe and that all of the neighbors used it too.

I continued the service, but after watching the pesticide fog settle over our yard a few times,

it troubled me to think my children would be running around in all those chemicals. I canceled the service, but the people there warned me that I didn't know what I was getting into.

Sure enough! Soon my porch floor was sticky with aphids that dripped from the ivy. My bent-grass lawn (which should never have been planted in my arid climate) was a mass of patchy fungus problems. Besides that, whiteflies had moved in on the camellias, and spider mites were everywhere.

Luckily, I met an entomologist in the neighborhood and mentioned my problem. Her im-

mediate response was, "You have a classic case of resurgence, or what we call pest flare-back." She told me that I could, with time, restore some sort of natural balance but that I would need to compensate for the fact

The indiscriminate spraying of pesticides can upset the natural balance of a garden for many years.

This beetle, making its way across an astilbe flower, is just one of the many interconnected insects present in any garden. Each has a specific role to play.

that all my neighbors continued to spray. She suggested I start my counterattack by luring beneficial insects into my yard with plants that provided them with nectar and pollen.

My entomologist friend explained to me that no matter what type you use, pesticides never kill every insect in an area, leaving some insects to reproduce. As a general rule, those insects that consume or suck sap from plants can reproduce very quickly, leaving gardeners to face a fast population explosion if there are no natural enemies around. On the other hand, predatory and parasitic insects (the good guys) reproduce slowly. Many of them also need access to pollen and nectar (usually in short supply in the average yard) at some stage of their life cycle.

That conversation provided my first clue to understanding that a balanced garden, in terms of insects, is a healthy garden. While my friend pointed me in the right direction, I still had a lot to learn. In fact, my first decade of stewardship of the garden was a period of significant stumbling around. In the short run I was able to cut my pesticide use because I was maintaining a landscape filled with lawn, vines, shrubs and trees—a much simpler proposition than true gardening. I overseeded the disease-prone bent grass with tough fescue and replaced the spider mite-infested azaleas. That helped, but I still felt compelled to spray the aphids on the ivy and put out

Unlike any front yard garden you've probably ever seen, Ros Creasy makes maximum use of every square inch of soil, filling it with bounty and beauty.

If you accept a little damage as a part of the natural scheme of things, you may be in for a surprise: This caterpillar will eventually become a beautiful black swallowtail butterfly.

poison bait for the ever-present snails. For a while a sort of uneasy truce held in my garden. By 1975, however, garden fever had set in with such vengeance that I attended college to get my landscape design degree.

I soon planted every vegetable and flower I could find and then the truce was over. My asparagus plants were overrun by asparagus beetles (a pest imported to this country from Europe in 1881); hornworms and bronze mites attacked my tomatoes; flea beetles tore through the eggplants; and numerous diseases disfigured the roses. And those snails were still lurking around.

I decided I would fight back, but only by using so-called organic pesticide. The problem is, organic pesticides usually kill both good insects and bad, so once again my garden's natural balance was upset. (At least organic pesticides are quick to degrade, unlike many of the persistent commercial pesticides.) For some time I continued, trying to force my garden to behave on my terms, with better or worse results.

A Silent Spring

In 1981, I witnessed something that helped solidify and reinforce my belief that a natural ecosystem has the best chance of thriving without a lot of intervention on the part of the gardener.

It was during the height of the Mediterranean fruit fly (*Ceratitis capitata*) invasion, a pest introduced from overseas that had the potential to devastate domestic orchard crops. The state of California responded by using helicopters to spray our county with malathion, a broad-spectrum pesticide.

What happened next was a terrible disruption of the natural cycle of predator and prey in my garden, as well as across the county. The malathion killed the medfly, but it also killed untold numbers of other garden insects—both good and bad.

Within weeks, the leaves of my vegetables and roses carried a veritable plague of aphids and whiteflies—so many that the plants looked wilted. I started to see all sorts of pest problems that I'd never seen before. There was also an eerie stillness in the night because the songs of the katydids and crickets were missing. Within months, there were no mockingbirds to be heard in my area either. Presumably, they left because their food sources were no longer around.

I knew that this was one gardening battle I was not going to win. I sadly pulled out most of my vegetable garden. Then I concentrated on repeatedly washing pests off my roses and fruit trees with strong streams of water from a hose while waiting for the return of the insects

We used to say "ladybug, ladybug, fly away home," but now wise gardeners want as many of these little pest-eating beetles as possible in their gardens.

with the "white hats." It took two years for the number of good insects to approach normal and it was three years before we heard a cricket again.

Discovering Beneficial Insects

In retrospect, the spraying was an eye-opening moment for me. I finally concluded the largest contribution I could make during my lifetime was to learn to garden organically and to share that knowledge with others. I also saw the real power of beneficial insects and it gave me a new dedication. Along the way, I learned a few things that have helped me nurture a strong garden ecosystem—tips that can help you too.

For instance, I found out that pest insects are the first ones to hatch in spring. Most predatory and parasitic insects don't hatch until there is food available. That's why I no longer spray the aphids on my ivy every spring, even with an organic pesticide, because I know that I would also

be killing the beneficial parasitic wasps hidden inside the aphid bodies and be starving the larvae of beneficial young syrphid flies, which feed on aphids.

Further, I now know that some of the most powerful beneficial insects, such as lacewings and syrphid flies, need nectar and pollen when they are larvae. That's why I now plant a feast of flowers in my garden designed just to feed these good guys. I've also found out that big showy flowers like dahlias, tea roses, gladiolus and the like, provide little sustenance for beneficials.

Instead, I line my flower beds with tiny nectar-rich flowers such as alyssum, species marigolds (*Tagetes* spp.) and zinnias. I also plant herbs all over my garden for their generous flowers and I let vegetables such as broccoli and mâche (a green also known as corn salad) flower as well. These measures are especially important in the spring when the hatching beneficials need the nectar most. I also provide a birdbath and bird

feeders in my garden, to encourage birds which help control my caterpillars.

In recent years a number of companies have begun selling beneficial insects in containers for release into home gardens. If only I'd had that option after the malathion spraying, I would have ordered lacewings to jump-start my garden. Lacewings are the most effective beneficial insects in terms of eliminating most garden pests. They can be purchased as egg cases and then placed in a garden. A nectar food spray is also available from nurseries to spray in the vicinity of the young larvae; this will encourage them to stay in your garden and work for you.

The Battle Continues

Of course, relying on natural balance to take care of all your insect problems in a garden has its limitations. Myriad pests from abroad have been brought into this country without their accompanying natural enemies. Japanese beetles, gypsy moths, fire ants and European brown snails run amok in our gardens because they have no natural predators. If you are forced to use a toxic chemical in a garden, it's usually for this type of pest. If you must use such a chemical, try to use a selective pesticide that will kill only the problem insect. Using a broad-spectrum pesticide will upset the insect balance in your garden. Always remember to read the label on any garden chemical, and follow the directions carefully.

Sometimes the weather is so extreme that the life cycle of your beneficial insects is disturbed, despite your best efforts. In addition, in our zeal for new, flashy plants for our gardens, we have often bred plants that are so weak that they must be propped up chemically with fertilizers and pesticides in order to have even a fighting chance.

Contrary to what a lot of us were brought up to believe, not all insects are pests—in fact, some, like this lacewing, are beneficial, helping the gardener control the "bad guys."

Even this little black ant has an important role in the big scheme of things: The ant pollinated the flower as it walked across its stamen, giving the plant the ability to reproduce itself.

Know Your Limits

Because I understand both what a garden in balance can and can't do, I've made my peace with the fact that I can't grow some plants. Sometimes it's because the pest that attacks the plant has no natural predators; other times, it's because I still haven't perfected the balance that lets predator and prey coexist while still leaving me a reasonable number of fairly healthy plants.

For instance, I can't plant eggplants here (they get flea beetles) nor fuchsias (fuchsia mites have been introduced to this country). The list goes on: no zonal geraniums or petunias (budworms) and no asparagus (asparagus beetles).

But I've also drawn my own personal line in the sand. I refuse to give up growing tomatoes even though they suffer annually from bronze mites. (I also have a few floribunda roses that I can't live without, even though they do get mildew, a fungal disease.) I help these two favorites out with a monthly sulfur spray to control them. I also use a dormant oil spray on my plum trees to con-

trol scale insects. When I absolutely must grow something that my persistent pests adore, I turn to noninvasive methods to repel them, such as using floating row covers, a fabric barrier that physically keeps the insects from my crops.

Creating a Balance

I'm learning more every day about the careful balance between predator and prey in a healthy garden. For instance, I used to have a terrible problem with thrips. Nothing I tried worked until I found that the problem was my drip irrigation system. The soil wasn't staying moist enough to encourage a soil-dwelling predator of thrips that feeds on the pest. I now keep the soil around my sweet peas and my roses moist and my plants are doing fine.

We don't know all the answers yet for controlling either

pests or disease. I don't know why I can't get my particular recurring insect problems under control, so it's evident that I'm still missing a few pieces of the puzzle. It may be something as simple as the fact that I still have to spray sometimes for disease and that upsets the balance in my garden.

There is still so much more to learn. For instance, some studies have shown that plants under stress seem more prone to pests. One theory says that stressed plants produce more carbohydrates and this in turn makes them more attractive to pests. The lesson? Healthy, strong, well-adapted plants in a garden may not even catch the pests' eyes. In addition, a cornucopia of new pest- and disease-resistant vegetable and flower varieties is available, giving us more weapons in the battle.

Gardening practices are changing quickly, and for the better. My guess is that soon, few of us will routinely ask, "Which chemical do I use and when do I spray?" Instead we'll say to ourselves, "What's out of balance here and what can I do to restore it?"

While certainly a thing of beauty, the four lined plant bug causes leaves and flowers of plants to become dwarfed and distorted. If you see any of these critters on your plants, remove and destroy them before they can create any big damage.

◆ CHAPTER 2 ◆
QUICK-SOLUTION CHART

T he chart on the following pages should be used as a guide for quickly identifying problems and cures in your garden. Each entry features an illustration of the pest or disease, its common hosts, and remedies, listed in order from the most benign—in terms of environmental impact—to the most extreme. If you catch a problem when it first appears, the simplest, lowest impact remedy will almost always do the job. That's why it's so important to get out there in your garden on a daily basis—not only to enjoy its pleasures, but to keep an eye out for the "bad guys" that can rob a garden of its beauty.

APHIDS

Symptoms

Clusters of tiny soft-bodied green or brownish insects visible on leaves—especially on new growth and developing buds. Eventually plants become weak, wilted, stunted or discolored. Blooms may become deformed or fall off. A shiny, sticky substance, known as "honeydew," may coat the leaves. Ants are attracted to the honeydew, as is a blackish mold.

Hosts

Wide variety of garden plants.

Cure

Start control by encouraging natural aphid enemies such as ladybugs, lacewings, syrphid flies, soldier beetles and parasitic wasps; plant small-flowered nectar plants, such as yarrow, dill and Queen Anne's lace. Wash aphid infestations off plants with a strong jet of water. Cradle tender growth in your hand while spraying to prevent damage. If infestation persists, spray plants with insecticidal soap or azadirachtin (see pages 142 and 144). Apply these treatments to both the tops and undersides of leaves. Chemical controls include insecticides containing pyrethrin, malathion or acephate (see pages 146-149).

ASTER YELLOWS

Symptoms

Stunted plants with yellowing, spindly stems. Flowers may be yellowish green and deformed.

Hosts

Garden chrysanthemum, cosmos, anemone, cornflower and other ornamental plants.

Cure

No cure. Remove and destroy infected plants (do not compost) to keep microorganisms from spreading to other plants.

BACTERIAL SOFT ROT

Symptoms

Leaf and stalk may rot at base, fall over, or not develop correctly. Bulbs affected will be soft and rotten, with a foul smell, and will probably fail to sprout.

Hosts

Hyacinth bulbs and rhizomatous iris.

Cure

No cure once infection is present. Remove and destroy all diseased plants. Plant in well-drained soil and do not overwater.

BACTERIAL WILT

Symptoms

Entire plant or just stems may wilt; foliage turns yellow and dies. When infected stems are cut, a milky white sap is produced; a knife touched to the sap and drawn away slowly will produce a fine thread of sap.

Hosts

Dianthus and other ornamental plants.

Cure

No cure once infection is present. Remove and destroy all infected plants. To avoid spreading the disease, dip tools in rubbing alcohol after pruning the infected plants. Do not overwater or crowd plants.

BASAL ROT

Symptoms

Necks of bulbs are soft and brown; inside leaves turn yellow. Plant may be stunted and die prematurely. White fungal growth may appear on the base of the bulb. Infected bulbs may not sprout at all.

Hosts

Flower bulbs.

Cure

No cure once infection is present. Remove and destroy infected plants/bulbs. Avoid problem by planting bulbs in well-drained soil. Do not plant healthy bulbs in areas where disease has been present.

BLACK SPOT

Symptoms

Black, irregular circles on the top of leaves. May cause leaves to turn yellow and drop prematurely.

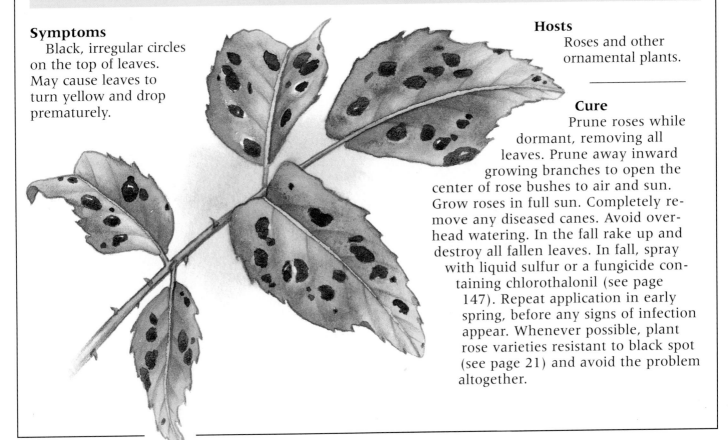

Hosts

Roses and other ornamental plants.

Cure

Prune roses while dormant, removing all leaves. Prune away inward growing branches to open the center of rose bushes to air and sun. Grow roses in full sun. Completely remove any diseased canes. Avoid overhead watering. In the fall rake up and destroy all fallen leaves. In fall, spray with liquid sulfur or a fungicide containing chlorothalonil (see page 147). Repeat application in early spring, before any signs of infection appear. Whenever possible, plant rose varieties resistant to black spot (see page 21) and avoid the problem altogether.

BLACK STEM ROT

Symptoms
  Blackening at base of stems, progressing up the plant.

Hosts
  Geraniums and other ornamental plants.

Cure
  Destroy infected plants. If grown in a container, dispose of soil. Dip all tools and pots in a solution of bleach and water (1 part bleach to 9 parts water) for one minute or more. Avoid the problem by using a sterilized, fast-draining potting mix, and don't over-water.

BLISTER BEETLE

Symptoms
  Chewed leaves; severe infestations cause leaves to drop.

Hosts
  Many ornamental plants.

Cure
  Start by removing damaged leaves; handpick and destroy beetles. If infestation persists, spray with insecticide containing rotenone, pyrethrum, carbaryl, acephate or malathion (see pages 142-149). Avoid future infestations with an application of beneficial parasitic nematodes, which will destroy the pupae and larvae before they can develop into damaging beetles (see page 150).

BRISTLY ROSE SLUGS

Symptoms
  Holes on leaves or skeletonized foliage. Flowers may be chewed and infested.

Hosts
  Roses.

Cure
  Handpick or use insecticidal soap. Dusting leaves with wood ash will also kill rose slugs. Promote natural predators such as beetles and parasitic wasps: Plant small-flowered nectar plants such as yarrow, dill and Queen Anne's lace.

BROWN CANKER

Symptoms
  In summer purplish spots appear on canes. In winter tan spots develop on canes.

Hosts
  Roses.

Cure
  Prune out any infected canes and destroy. Dip pruning shears in rubbing alcohol to prevent spreading disease to healthy plants.

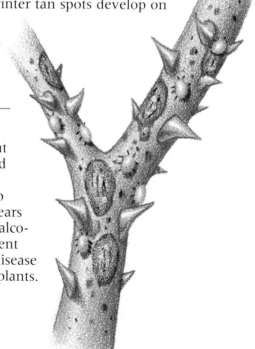

BUD ROT AND CANNA ROT

Symptoms
  Newly opened leaves may be partially or entirely black, possibly covered with white spots. Older leaves may be covered with yellow or brown spots.

Hosts
  Cannas.

Cure
  There are no cures. Remove and destroy any infected leaves and flowers. Severely diseased plants should be completely removed and destroyed; this includes the surrounding soil.

BULB MITES

Symptoms
  Plants grow slowly; leaves turn speckled yellow. Bulbs may rot in soil or in storage.

Hosts
  Wide variety of flowering bulbs.

Cure
  Remove and destroy any soft and rotting corms. Control these pests with a spray of malathion (see page 149).

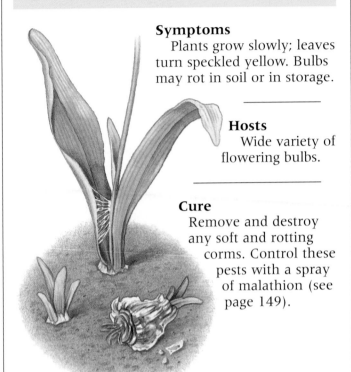

BULB ROT

Symptoms
  Sparse and stunted foliage. Bulbs may be covered with white, pink or gray mold.

Hosts
  Wide variety of flowering bulbs.

Cure
  Remove and destroy all diseased plants and bulbs. Dip clean, healthy bulbs in a fungicide containing captan before storing; follow label directions (see page 146). Store bulbs in a cool, dry place with good air circulation.

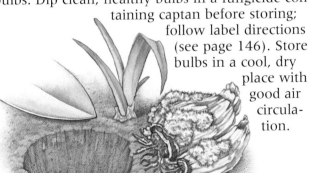

BURDOCK BORERS

Symptoms
  Chewed leaves; stalks may wilt and fall to the ground.

Hosts
  Larkspur.

Cure
  Slit stem lengthwise and remove the borer. Tape stem together with masking tape until it heals. If this treatment does not work, remove and destroy dying plants.

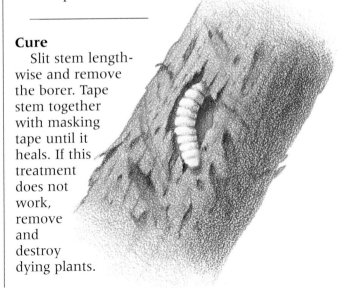

CABBAGE LOOPERS

Symptoms

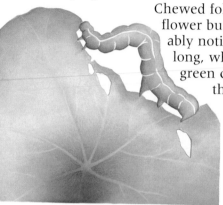

Chewed foliage and flower buds. You'll probably notice $1^1/_2$-inch-long, white-striped, green caterpillars as they feed.

Hosts

Calendula, carnation and nasturtium.

Cure

Remove all plant debris and weeds in autumn. At the first sign of attack, spray with Btk, especially effective on young caterpillars (see page 143). If infestation persists, spray with an insecticide containing pyrethrum, rotenone or carbaryl (see pages 146-149). Respray 10 to 14 days later if reinfestation occurs.

CATERPILLARS

Symptoms

Chewed leaves and sizable holes.

Hosts

Many annuals and perennials.

Cure

Start control by handpicking and destroying caterpillars. Spray with Bt or azadirachtin (see pages 142-143). Prevent the problem by cultivating the soil in fall to kill overwintering soil-borne pupae.

CERCOSPORA LEAF SPOT

Symptoms

Leaves show white spots surrounded by a red band; centers of spots eventually fall out.

Hosts

Calendula, lavender, geranium and other ornamental plants.

Cure

Remove and destroy infected plants. Wash hands and tools before touching other plants. If infection is severe, remove and discard any soil that roots have touched. Remove all plant debris in fall and use an organic mulch after planting plants in spring. Provide wide spacing between plants for good air circulation.

COLORADO POTATO BEETLES

Symptoms
Chewed leaves and stems. Whole plant may be devoured by brick-red grubs and yellow-and-black striped beetles.

Hosts
Many ornamental plants.

Cure
Try handpicking beetles and applying thick organic mulch first. If infestation continues, apply Bt or Bt *san diego* strain (see page 143). Last resort: Spray with insecticide containing pyrethrum, rotenone, azadirachtin or carbaryl (see pages 142-149). In fall, remove all garden debris and cultivate beds to prevent infestation in next year's garden. To avoid the problem in the future, make an application of beneficial nematodes (see page 150).

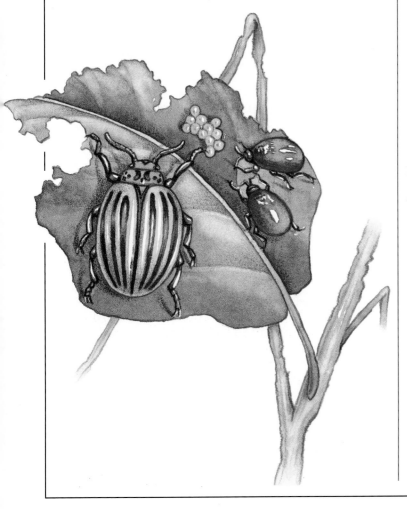

COLUMBINE BORERS

Symptoms
Stems break and leaves wilt. Small round holes appear on stems or crowns.

Hosts
Columbine.

Cure
Cut off and dispose of infested stems. At first sign of attack, spray with Bt (see page 143); if you wait until the borers have entered the stems, spray will be ineffective.

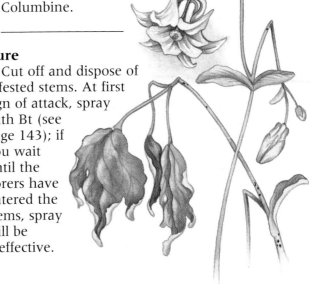

COMMON STALK BORER

Symptoms
Stems break, leaves wilt and plants suddenly collapse. Leaves are chewed and ragged. Small round holes appear on stems or crowns.

Hosts
A variety of annuals and perennials.

Cure
Remove and destroy all infested plants. Spray Bt before borers enter the stems (see page 143). Last resort: Spray with insecticide containing carbaryl (see pages 146-147). Remove all weeds and garden debris in fall to help prevent future infestation.

CROWN GALLS

Symptoms

Hard, rough, irregularly shaped, tumor-like growths at base of plants, ranging from pea-size to tennis ball-size.

Hosts

Shrubs, vines, roses and a variety of annuals and perennials.

Cure

Infected plants cannot be cured, but galls rarely kill plants. Prune out and destroy galled stems. Sterilize pruning shears with rubbing alcohol after each cut. Remove and destroy seriously infected plants.

CUTWORMS

Symptoms

Chewed leaves and seedlings eaten off at ground level.

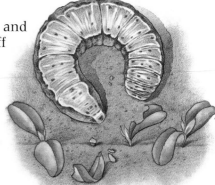

Hosts

Almost any young transplant.

Cure

Encourage natural predators such as beneficial soil nematodes, parasitoid wasps, ground beetles, soldier beetles, predatory stink bugs and tachinid flies. Use cutworm collars, especially around young transplants (see illustration, page 151). Commercial controls include Bt baited granules and carbaryl bait (see pages 143-149). To help prevent infestation, cultivate beds in fall and spring to expose and kill the cutworm larvae. Avoid the problem in the future by solarizing the soil (see page 151).

DAMPING OFF

Symptoms

Seedlings may not appear, or may grow only 1 inch, then wilt and fall over.

Hosts

Seedling transplants.

Cure

If you grow seedlings indoors, avoid damping off by providing as much light and air circulation as possible. Use a sterilized, fast-draining soil mix to start seedlings and water carefully, letting soil dry slightly between waterings. A thin layer of sand or perlite on top of the soil mix will also help avoid the problem. Do not overfertilize seedlings.

DIAMONDBACK MOTHS

Symptoms
Irregular holes in leaves and squiggly, tan lines in flowers.

Hosts
Carnation, candytuft and nasturtium.

Cure
Handpick and destroy caterpillars and their cocoons. Make weekly applications of insecticidal soap as long as caterpillars are present (see page 144). For persistent infestations, apply Bt or pyrethrin to the foliage (see page 143). To help prevent future problems, thoroughly clean up plant debris in fall and cultivate the soil.

DIDYMELLINA LEAF SPOT

Symptoms
Brown spots, $^1/_8$ to $^1/_4$ inch in diameter, appear on leaves. Spots have reddish borders and later may turn yellow.

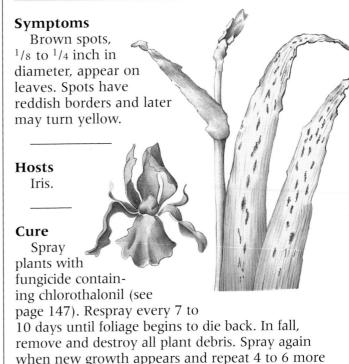

Hosts
Iris.

Cure
Spray plants with fungicide containing chlorothalonil (see page 147). Respray every 7 to 10 days until foliage begins to die back. In fall, remove and destroy all plant debris. Spray again when new growth appears and repeat 4 to 6 more times at intervals of 7 to 10 days.

DOWNY MILDEW

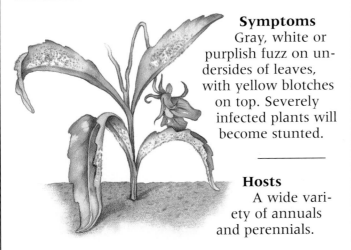

Symptoms
Gray, white or purplish fuzz on undersides of leaves, with yellow blotches on top. Severely infected plants will become stunted.

Hosts
A wide variety of annuals and perennials.

Cure
Prune and destroy all infected foliage. If the problem persists, apply a fungicide containing copper, sulfur or a Bordeaux mixture (see pages 142-145). Help avoid the problem by watering plants in the morning, providing wide spacing to promote good air circulation. In fall, remove all debris from around plants.

EARWIGS

Symptoms
Tender seedlings' tips are chewed.

Hosts
A wide variety of ornamental plants.

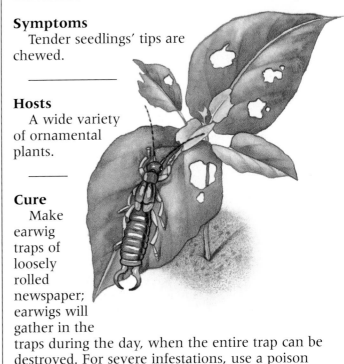

Cure
Make earwig traps of loosely rolled newspaper; earwigs will gather in the traps during the day, when the entire trap can be destroyed. For severe infestations, use a poison bait formulated specifically for earwigs.

EUROPEAN CORN BORERS

Symptoms
Leaves show small "shot holes" and stems may have holes where borers have entered.

Hosts
A variety of annuals and perennials.

Cure
Begin control by handpicking and destroying borers. For severe infestations, apply beneficial nematodes, baited Bt granules, rotenone or carbaryl (see pages 143-147). Remove all plant debris and weeds in the fall to help prevent future infestations.

FALL WEB WORMS

Symptoms
Chewed leaves, buds and blossoms. With severe infestations, whole branches can be defoliated. Plants become covered with white webbing.

Hosts
Roses and other ornamental plants.

Cure
Attract parasitic wasps and other beneficial insects by growing small-flowered nectar plants such as alyssum, scabiosa and yarrow. Prune and destroy infected foliage. Oil sprays, Bt and products containing malathion, carbaryl or acephate will control severe infestations (see pages 143-149).

FOUR LINED PLANT BUGS

Symptoms
Leaves and flowers are distorted or dwarfed. Yellow, tan or brown spots may develop in early summer.

Hosts
Geraniums and other annuals and perennials.

Cure
Begin control by handpicking and destroying bugs. Spray insecticidal soap on undersides of leaves every third day until pests disappear (see page 144). Avoid future problems: Clean up garden debris in spring and fall.

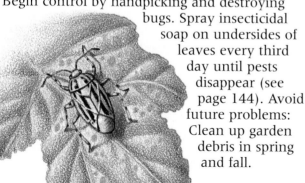

FOXGLOVE ANTHRACNOSE

Symptoms
Small, irregular-shaped, light-brown to purplish brown spots, $1/8$ inch in diameter. Severely infected areas turn yellow, shrivel, and drop.

Hosts
Foxgloves.

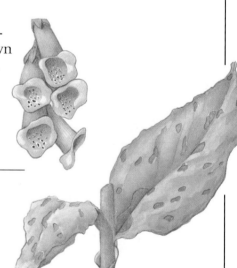

Cure
Pick off and destroy infected leaves. If the problem persists, spray with a fungicide containing chlorothalonil (see page 147). Avoid future problems by removing and destroying all plant debris in fall. Avoid overhead watering, which spreads the disease; allow the soil to dry out between waterings.

FULLER ROSE BEETLES

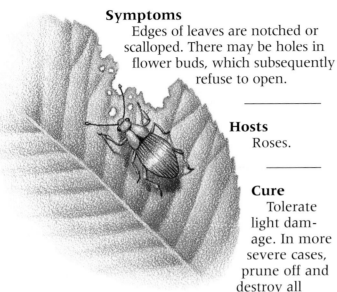

Symptoms
Edges of leaves are notched or scalloped. There may be holes in flower buds, which subsequently refuse to open.

Hosts
Roses.

Cure
Tolerate light damage. In more severe cases, prune off and destroy all infested foliage and flower buds. Avoid the problem in the future with an application of beneficial nematodes (*Steinernema carpocapsae* and *Heterorhabditis heliothidis*) to the soil around roses (see page 150).

FUSARIUM BULB ROT

Symptoms
Leaves turn yellow; plant is stunted and dies prematurely. Bulbs in storage develop purple-brown areas of decay. White fungus strands may appear on bulbs.

Hosts
A wide variety of bulbs.

Cure
No treatment once infection is present. Remove and destroy diseased plants and bulbs. Dig up and discard soil surrounding infected bulbs for 6 inches in all directions. When digging bulbs, do so carefully to prevent wounds, which are points of entry for the disease. Do not replant healthy bulbs in area where diseased plants have previously grown.

FUSARIUM WILT

Symptoms
Leaves curl and stems wilt. Leaves drop prematurely.

Hosts
A wide variety of annuals, perennials and vegetables.

Cure
Remove and discard infected plants at the first sign of infection. Add agricultural lime to raise soil alkalinity to pH 6.5 to 7.5. Avoid overwatering.

FUSARIUM YELLOWS

Symptoms
Foliage and flower are stunted, and may be small and faded. Leaf tips turn yellow. Disease may spread through entire plant, eventually killing it. Plants affected with fusarium yellows will reveal rotten roots when pulled from the ground.

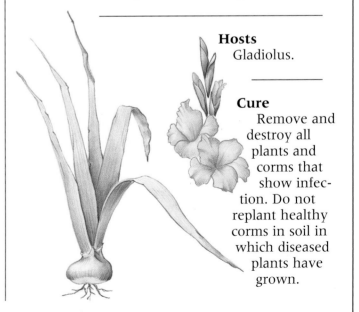

Hosts
Gladiolus.

Cure
Remove and destroy all plants and corms that show infection. Do not replant healthy corms in soil in which diseased plants have grown.

GLADIOLUS THRIPS

Symptoms

Leaves turn brown and die. Silvery white streaks on flowers and foliage. Tiny blackish brown winged insects appear on plants during mornings and late afternoons.

Hosts

Gladiolus.

Cure

Knock thrips off with a blast of water. Water plants regularly during dry spells. Attract parasitic wasps, soldier beetles, green lacewings and other beneficial insects by planting small-flowered nectar plants including alyssum and scabiosa. For severe infestations, spray infested plants with insecticide containing acephate (see page 146). If the problem persists, respray at intervals of 7 to 10 days.

GRASSHOPPERS

Symptoms

Tender seedlings will be the first casualties to grasshoppers. Eventually large holes will appear around the edges of leaves of all types of plants as the grasshoppers continue their frenzied feeding.

Hosts

A wide variety of ornamental plants.

Cure

If infestation is not large, handpick and destroy insects. Attract birds, which eat grasshoppers, by providing water and shrubby nesting places. Till the soil in autumn to expose and destroy grasshopper eggs. For severe infestations, spray with an insecticide containing neem, carbaryl, malathion or acephate (see pages 142-149). Problems with crickets in the future can be avoided with an application of *Nosema locustae* (see page 145), but it works best when applied over a wide area as opposed to just one yard.

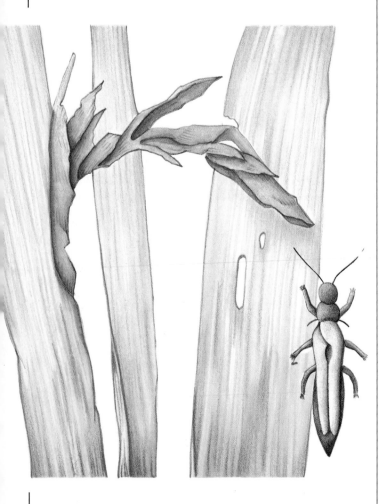

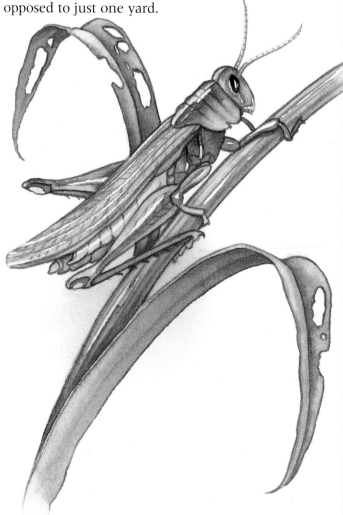

GRAY MOLD

Symptoms
   Lesions covered with gray spores appear on leaves, stems, blossoms or fruit.

Hosts
   A wide variety of annuals, perennials and bulbs.

Cure
   Remove and destroy all infected plant parts. To prevent further infection, spray with a fungicide containing chlorothalonil (see page 147). Repeat spray every 5 to 7 days until flowers bloom.

IRON DEFICIENCY

Symptoms
   The leaves of a plant will start to turn pale green, and will eventually yellow. The veins of the plant will still be green. In some severe cases the leaves become totally chlorotic.

Hosts
   Azalea, camellia, gardenia and rhododendron.

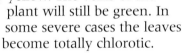

Cure
   Start with an acid-forming mulch such as pine straw or shredded bark. Use a fertilizer designed to acidify soil, or apply sulfur. If the problem persists, test the soil's pH to see if it is too alkaline for the plants there; a pH above 7.5 is too high. Soil test kits are available at garden centers and your local Cooperative Extension Office. A soil test done by the latter will tell you exactly how much additive your soil needs. Work only at shallow soil levels to avoid further plant stress.

IRIS BORER

Symptoms
   Dark streaks, water-soaked spots and possible slits in new leaves. Leaves have pinholes or are chewed. Rotting leaf bases.

Hosts
   Iris.

Cure
   Remove and destroy all infested plants and rhizomes. When the borers are present, introduce beneficial nematodes (*Steinernema carpocapsae* and *Heterorhabditis heliothidis*) to the garden, following label directions carefully (see page 150). To disrupt the borer's natural life cycle, cover the soil around the rhizomes with landscape fabric (usually used to prevent weeds) to keep the borers from reaching the soil.

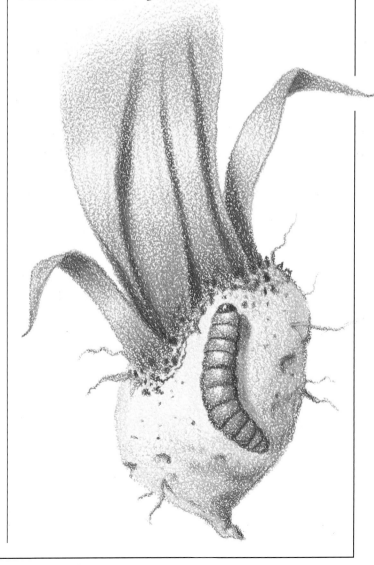

JAPANESE BEETLES

Symptoms
Leaves and flowers chewed in lacy pattern.

Hosts
Many ornamental plants.

Cure
If infestation is not large, handpick and destroy insects. For larger infestations use insecticidal soap or spray with azadirachtin (see pages 142-145). As a last resort, spray with insecticide containing pyrethrum, rotenone, acephate, carbaryl or malathion (see pages 146-149). To avoid future problems with beetles, apply parasitic nematodes or milky spores to soil (see page 150).

LACE BUGS

Symptoms
Foliage appears speckled, splotched or striped with bleached-looking spots. Shiny, hard black droplets show up on the undersides of damaged leaves.

Hosts
Many ornamental plants.

Cure
Pick off and destroy infected leaves. Start by handpicking and destroying insects, or spray with insecticidal soap (see page 144). Be sure to spray both tops and undersides of leaves. If infestation persists, spray with an insecticide containing pyrethrum, malathion, carbaryl or acephate (see pages 146-149). To avoid future problems, attract lace bug's natural insect enemies with plantings of alyssum and dill.

LEAFHOPPERS

Symptoms
Stippled and/or yellowing leaves.

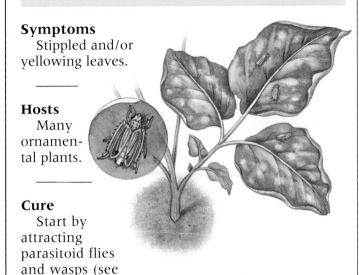

Hosts
Many ornamental plants.

Cure
Start by attracting parasitoid flies and wasps (see page 150). Use insecticidal soap or light horticultural oil, making sure to spray both tops and undersides of leaves (see pages 142-145). Remove nearby weeds that harbor eggs and insects. Last resort: Spray with insecticide containing pyrethrum, rotenone, acephate, carbaryl or malathion (see pages 146-149).

LEAF MINERS

Symptoms
Light tan, winding trails or blotches on or in leaves. Plants may be stunted or killed.

Hosts
A wide variety of annuals and perennials.

Cure
Pick and destroy affected leaves. Natural controls include attracting parasitoid wasps (see page 150). Chemical controls include insecticides containing acephate (see page 146). After initial spray, repeat two more times at weekly intervals. Avoid future damage by treating the soil with beneficial nematodes (see page 150).

LEAF ROLLER

Symptoms
Leaves rolled into tubes, tied with fine, sticky webbing; when unrolled, you'll notice leaf-eating caterpillars inside.

Hosts
A wide variety of ornamental plants.

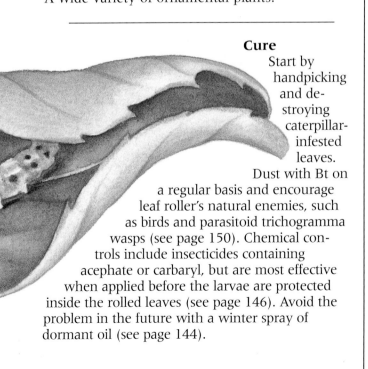

Cure
Start by handpicking and destroying caterpillar-infested leaves. Dust with Bt on a regular basis and encourage leaf roller's natural enemies, such as birds and parasitoid trichogramma wasps (see page 150). Chemical controls include insecticides containing acephate or carbaryl, but are most effective when applied before the larvae are protected inside the rolled leaves (see page 146). Avoid the problem in the future with a winter spray of dormant oil (see page 144).

LEAF SCORCH

Symptoms
Leaf tips may be brown. Brown crescent or semi-circular areas develop along leaf edges. The lower leaves area affected first.

Hosts
Lilies and some shrubs.

Cure
Add ground dolomitic limestone to decrease acidity, and apply a balanced fertilizer.

MEALY BUGS

Symptoms
White, woolly, sticky specks and black mold on leaves. Leaves eventually turn yellow and drop.

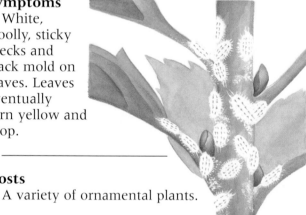

Hosts
A variety of ornamental plants.

Cure
Start control by spraying mealy bugs off with a strong blast of water. If infestation persists, spray with insecticidal soap (see page 144). Chemical controls including insecticides containing azadirachtin, pyrethrum, malathion or acephate (see pages 142-149). To avoid problems in the future, attract beneficial insects, such as parasitic wasps, by planting nectar plants like alyssum and dill.

LEAF SPOT

Symptoms
Leaves have small, yellow to dark brown spots with purplish black sunken areas; grayish brown dead areas eventually develop in the center of the spot. Leaf tissues around spot may turn yellow. Lesions develop on stems, especially at bases. The entire plant may eventually wilt and die.

Hosts
Many annuals and perennials.

Cure
Remove and destroy leaves as soon as possible. Do not compost. Clean tools with rubbing alcohol after pruning infected plants. If totally infected, remove and destroy plant. Water plants in the morning so the foliage has a chance to dry before nightfall. Space plants widely to allow good air circulation. Avoid wetting the foliage when watering. Fertilize well throughout the growing season and remove all garden debris regularly. If disease persists, spray weekly with sulfur or a fungicide containing chlorothalonil (see pages 145 and 147).

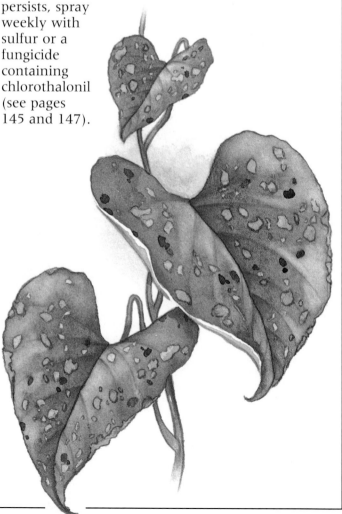

MOSAIC VIRUS

Symptoms
Leaves distorted or smaller than normal, mottled with spots of yellow, white or brown. In some cases the foliage develops yellow rings.

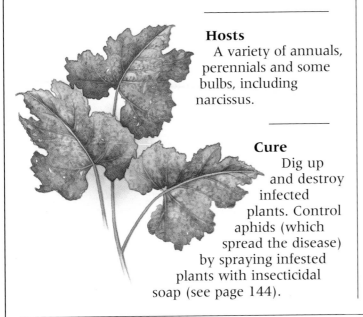

Hosts
A variety of annuals, perennials and some bulbs, including narcissus.

Cure
Dig up and destroy infected plants. Control aphids (which spread the disease) by spraying infested plants with insecticidal soap (see page 144).

NARCISSUS STREAK

Symptoms
Leaves and flowers have pale streaks and may wilt.

Hosts
Daffodils.

Cure
Knock off disease-carrying insects with a strong blast of water, or spray infected plants with insecticidal soap (see page 144).

OEDEMA

Symptoms
Watery blisters on leaves which eventually turn brown or rust colored.

Hosts
A variety of ornamental plants.

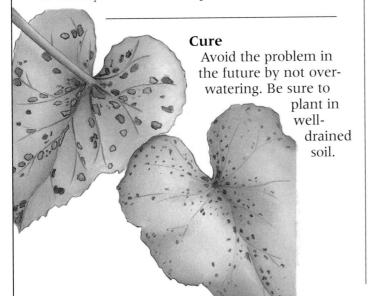

Cure
Avoid the problem in the future by not over-watering. Be sure to plant in well-drained soil.

PHLOX PLANT BUGS

Symptoms
Leaves, shoots and flowers may be stunted or deformed. Young leaves and buds are chewed.

Hosts
Phlox.

Cure
Start control by hand-picking bugs and nymphs. Continue control with an insecticidal soap spray or light horticultural oil (see page 144). Or spray with an insecticide containing azadirachtin (see page 142).

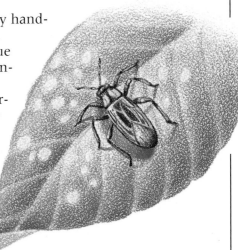

PHYTOPHTHORA BLIGHT

Symptoms
New plant shoots wilt and darken; eventually the whole plant shrivels and turns brown. Affected plants will be easy to pull from the ground.

Hosts
Peonies.

Cure
Dig up and destroy infected plants. To avoid spreading the disease, wash hands and sterilize tools with rubbing alcohol after working with infected plants. To help avoid the disease in the future, do not overwater plants and do not water from overhead. Grow plants in well-drained soil and remove all plant debris in the fall.

POWDERY MILDEW

Symptoms
Grayish, powdery-white coating appears on leaves, flowers and stems. Plants usually do not die, but infected leaves eventually turn yellow.

Hosts
A variety of annuals and perennials.

Cure
Dig up and destroy severely infected plants. To prevent future outbreaks, spray with baking soda. To make baking soda spray, dissolve 1 teaspoon baking soda in 1 quart warm water; add 1 teaspoon insecticidal soap to make the solution stick to the leaves. Use at intervals of 10-12 days to protect new growth. Remove plant debris in the fall.

ROOT NEMATODES

Symptoms
Leaves of affected plants will curl and may eventually yellow. Plant can be pulled out of ground easily. Knots may be visible on roots.

Hosts
Many annuals, perennials and bulbs.

Cure
Water and fertilize weak plants. Make regular additions of compost to garden beds which creates good conditions for beneficial organisms that attack nematodes.

ROOT ROT

Symptoms
Leaves and stems turn yellow, wilt and die. The lower leaves and stems may be soft and rotted. White fungal strands may grow around the bases of plants.

Hosts
Many ornamental plants.

Cure
Remove and destroy infected plants and soil immediately surrounding the roots. Avoid the problem by improving the soil drainage with regular additions of an organic soil amendment, such as compost. Avoid overwatering. If this disease persists, you may have to start new disease-free plants in a different garden location.

ROSE BUDWORMS

Symptoms

Leaves skeletonized and covered with webs. Buds and blossoms may be chewed.

Hosts

Roses.

Cure

Start control by handpicking and destroying worms. Encourage the worm's natural enemies, such as ladybugs, lacewings, syrphid flies, soldier beetles and parasitoid wasps, by planting small-flowered nectar plants, including yarrow, dill and Queen Anne's lace. If infestation persists, spray infested plants with Bt (see page 143).

ROSE LEAF CURL

Symptoms

Mottling, streaking or oddly shaped patterns develop on leaves. Foliage curls; plants are stunted.

Hosts

Roses.

Cure

Remove and destroy infected plants. Spray with insecticidal soap or light horticultural oil to control aphids and leafhoppers, which spread the disease (see page 144).

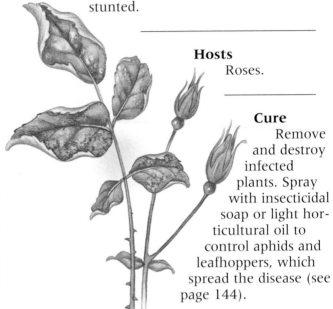

ROSE MIDGES

Symptoms

Buds and shoot tips turn black and shrivel. Tiny white maggots are visible.

Hosts

Roses.

Cure

Remove and destroy all infested plant parts on a daily basis until no more are seen. Avoid future problems by clearing away leaf litter, weeds or any debris where the larvae or adults may hide.

ROSE MOSAIC

Symptoms

Mottling or oddly shaped patterns on leaves. Foliage curls and plants are stunted.

Hosts

Roses.

Cure

Remove and destroy infected plants. Use insecticidal soap or light horticultural oil to control aphids and leafhoppers, which spread the disease (see page 144).

RUST

Symptoms
Leaves and stems have red or orange powdery spots and streaks, followed by yellow or dark splotches on tops.

Hosts
Many ornamental plants, including roses and herbs.

Cure
Remove and destroy infected leaves. Spray infected leaves with sulfur (see page 145). Avoid overhead watering. Water early in the day so plants will dry out before nightfall. Space or thin plants for good air circulation. Avoid splashing water on the foliage. Remove and compost all garden debris in the fall.

SCALE

Symptoms
Leaves are yellowed or distorted, sticky honeydew on leaves. Bump-like scales appear on leaves or stems.

Hosts
Many ornamental plants.

Cure
Physically scrape scale off stems with a plastic scouring pad. Prune off heavily encrusted canes or stems. Apply horticultural oil to smother the insects (see page 144). During the brief period when scale is in its crawler stage, spray with an insecticide containing pyrethrum (see page 149). Attract beneficial insects by planting small flowered nectar plants like alyssum, scabiosa and yarrow.

SLUGS AND SNAILS

Symptoms
Large holes in leaves and stems; whole plants may be defoliated. Shiny slime trails are on foliage or surrounding soil.

Hosts
Many ornamental plants, especially young, tender transplants.

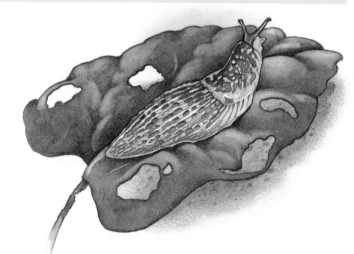

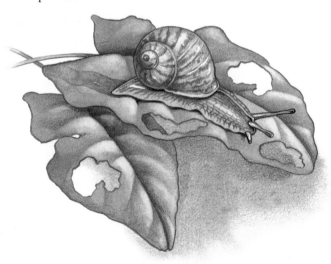

Cure
Handpick and destroy. Encircle plants with copper strips (available at nurseries and garden centers). Sprinkle planting beds with a bait containing iron phosphate or a chemical bait containing metaldehyde or methiocarb (see pages 145 and 148). Encourage natural enemies of snails and slugs: birds, toads, salamanders and predaceous ground beetles. Chickens and ducks are also efficient snail hunters.

SPIDER MITES

Symptoms
Flowers and leaves turn yellow, bronze or speckled. Fine webbing may appear on undersides of leaves. Affected leaves may drop prematurely.

Hosts
Many ornamental plants.

Cure
Knock mites off with a strong stream of water. Apply light horticultural oil to smother. If infestation persists, spray with insecticidal soap or pyrethrum (see pages 144 and 149). Avoid the problem by attracting beneficial insects by growing small-flowered nectar plants such as alyssum and dill.

SPITTLE BUG

Symptoms
White, frothy foam is clustered between leaves and stems. Small green insects under froth feeding on plant. Plants may be stunted.

Hosts
Annuals, perennials and herbs.

Cure
Knock spittle bugs off with a strong stream of water. If you have a heavy infestation, spray with malathion or acephate (see pages 146-148).

STEM ROT

Symptoms
Wilting of leaves, sometimes suddenly. Lower leaves and stems may rot.

Hosts
Calendula, carnation, geranium, poinsettia, sunflower.

Cure
If infection is not severe, some plants may be saved by merely decreasing irrigation. If this disease infects container-grown plants, remove the plant and soil, discard, and wash pots with mixture of one part bleach, nine parts water, for 30 minutes. Replant in fresh soil.

TARNISHED PLANT BUGS

Symptoms
Leaf surfaces will be speckled with yellow or brown spots. Spots of excrement on leaf undersides.

Hosts
Many ornamental plants.

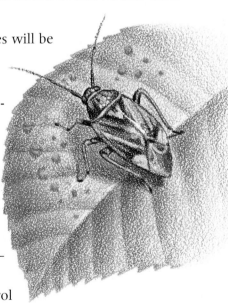

Cure
Begin control by handpicking and destroying the bugs. Continue control with an insecticidal soap spray or an insecticide containing malathion or carbaryl (see pages 146 and 148). Avoid the problem in the future by attracting beneficial insects by planting small-flowered nectar plants.

TOBACCO BUDWORMS

Symptoms
Healthy plants suddenly have small holes in leaves and buds. Blossoms may be chewed, and dark-colored droppings may be present.

Hosts
Calendula, nicotiana, petunia, ageratum, geraniums and penstemons.

Cure
Handpick and destroy worms. Remove dried-up buds and flowers that may harbor the budworms. If infestation continues, spray with Bt or an insecticide containing acephate or carbaryl (see pages 143 and 146).

TOMATO HORNWORMS

Symptoms
Buds, leaves, flowers and even fruit may be chewed to tatters or eaten entirely.

Hosts
Datura, nicotiana, petunia and tomatoes.

Cure
Handpick and destroy the hornworms. Btk is effective on small larvae (see page 143). Attract the hornworm's natural enemies—parasitoid wasps and birds. If infestation is heavy, control with an insecticide containing pyrethrum, rotenone, azadirachtin or carbaryl (see pages 142-149).

TULIP BREAKING VIRUS

Symptoms
Leaves become mottled with light and dark green blotches. Flower petals have bleached streaks.

Hosts
Tulips and lilies.

Cure
Dig up and destroy severely infected plants. Spray with insecticidal soap to control the insects that spread the disease (see page 144). Keep plants well watered and fertilized to help them resist insect attacks.

VERTICILLIUM WILT

Symptoms
Wilted foliage begins on the lower part of the plant and progresses up the stem. Leaves may develop yellow patches that eventually turn brown.

Hosts
Many ornamental plants.

Cure
Dig up and destroy diseased plants. If infection continues, plant susceptible plants in containers or other garden locations. Avoid the problem in the future by solarizing the planting beds where verticillium wilt has been a problem (see page 151).

VIOLET SAWFLIES

Symptoms
Leaves are skeletonized—only veins and remnants of leaf tissue are left.

Hosts
Pansies and violets.

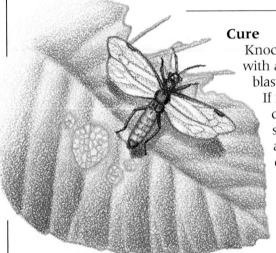

Cure
Knock off larvae with a strong blast of water. If infestation continues, spray with an insecticidal soap (see page 144).

WEEVILS

Symptoms
Holes appear in leaves and flowers. Some stems and leaves may be sheared off.

Hosts
Many annuals, perennials and bulbs.

Cure
Collect and destroy weevils by surrounding plant with cloth, shaking bugs into cloth, then destroy. If infestation continues, use an insecticide containing azadirachtin, rotenone, pyrethrum or acephate (see pages 142-149). Avoid the problem in the future with an application of beneficial nematodes (see page 150).

WHITEFLIES

Symptoms
Tiny winged insects feed on undersides of leaves. Leaves have spots of sticky, clear honeydew and may be mottled or turn yellow.

Hosts
Many annuals, perennials and bulbs.

Cure
Spray plants with insecticidal soap or light horticultural oil when whiteflies are first noticed (see page 144). Be sure to spray both the tops and undersides of leaves. If infestation continues, use an insecticide containing azadirachtin, acephate or malathion (see pages 142-149). Avoid the problem by attracting beneficial insects: Plant small-flowered nectar plants such as alyssum and dill.

❧ CHAPTER 3 ❧

ENCYCLOPEDIA OF PLANTS

This chapter contains detailed information on 65 favorite flowering plants—the most likely pests and diseases to attack each plant, specific remedies, and how to avoid problems in the first place. Where remedies are recommended, you'll be asked to consult Chapter Four, which begins on page 138, for more information on individual controls. When using any insecticide or fungicide, be sure to read and follow all label directions—for the health of your plants as well as the environment. The good news is, if you give a plant what it needs in terms of location and care, it will reward you with minimum problems and maximum beauty.

Achillea
YARROW

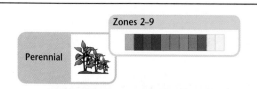

Perennial • Zones 2–9

Thrips

About the only insects to attack yarrow are thrips. Thrips damage appears as silvery or brown spots or streaking on leaves and flowers. Start by knocking thrips off with a strong blast of water. If thrips persist, use an insecticidal soap or azadirachtin (see pages 142 and 144).

Powdery Mildew

Thriving in hot, dry locations, yarrow will occasionally be bothered by powdery mildew if growing conditions turn humid. Although the disease is not fatal, its signature powdery white coating on foliage and flowers is unattractive. Remove and destroy any infected plants. Prevent further outbreaks of powdery mildew with a spray of liquid sulfur or baking soda (see pages 143 and 145).

Achillea is a very tolerant plant, seemingly thriving on neglect, plenty of sun, and well-drained soil.

Ageratum
FLOSSFLOWER

Annual • All Zones

Caterpillars

Two caterpillars—tobacco budworms and corn earworms—eat holes in ageratum leaves and flower buds. Natural controls include Bt, Btk and azadirachtin (see pages 142–143). Encourage the presence of the caterpillar's natural enemy, the parasitic wasp, with the wasp's favorite host plants (see page 150). Chemical controls include products containing acephate or carbaryl.

Leafrollers and Leaftiers

Rolled ageratum leaves, usually with some spiderweb-like material around them, indicate leafrollers and/or leaftiers. If you unroll the leaves, you'll probably find small caterpillars, only $1/2$ to $3/4$ inch long, lurking inside. Because the rolled leaf protects the caterpillars from sprays, the easiest, most effective solution is to simply pick off the affected leaves and dispose of them.

Spider Mites

Telltale signs of spider mites are white, yellow or reddish specks on leaves, and a fine webbing on their undersides. These minute pests suck sap from leaves and are particularly troublesome during extended periods of hot, dry weather. Avoid problems with spider mites by keeping ageratum consistently watered. Eliminate spider mites with a strong blast of water to the leaves. Other controls include insecticidal soap (see pages 144 and 147).

Whiteflies

If your ageratum plants are lacking in vigor, pale, and have clouds of very small white insects fly up when the leaves are disturbed, you've got an infestation of whiteflies. To control, either use an insecticidal soap or light horticultural oil (see page 144), or simply blast the whiteflies off the plants with a strong spray of water. For severe infestations, use an insecticide containing acephate or malathion (see pages 146 and 148).

Gray Mold

About the only common disease of ageratum is gray mold, which starts out as brown spots on leaves and stems; spots eventually become covered with brown or gray fuzzy mold. Infected plants diminish in vigor and ultimately die. To avoid problems, plant ageratum in a full-sun location in rich soil. In regions with a cool, damp growing season, wise gardeners avoid ageratum altogether.

Good air circulation around plants reduces the chances for disease, so don't overcrowd plants and don't water ageratum using an overhead spray which spreads the disease. Like any other disease, once gray mold appears, present damage cannot be eliminated, but future infection can be prevented. Remove and destroy any affected plants; avoid touching healthy plants with infected foliage. To avoid future problems with gray mold, spray plants with a fungicide containing maneb or chlorothalonil (see pages 147-148) once every 7 to 10 days.

Ageratum is favored for its unique, fuzzy blue flowers, but also comes in shades of pink and purple. Provide full fun to partial shade and evenly moist soil for best results.

Alcea
HOLLYHOCK

Biennial or short-lived perennial

Zones 2–9

Japanese Beetles

Leaves chewed, leaving nothing but the veins, indicate the presence of Japanese beetles. You'll want to catch these pests early, as they can do a lot of damage in a short while. Insecticidal soap will control Japanese beetles, and is especially effective when combined with milky spores, which kill the grubs of the beetles (see page 144). Chemical controls include products containing acephate, carbaryl or malathion (see pages 146 and 148).

Leaf Spot

Different-sized spots on hollyhock leaves—in shades of brown, black, purple or yellow—are a sure sign of leaf spot. Best bet is to cut off and discard any damaged foliage (or whole plants) as soon as possible. Water plants early in the day to allow foliage to dry before evening, and avoid wetting the foliage. If you use pruning shears to remove diseased foliage, dip the blades in rubbing alcohol before reuse.

Rust

The most common disease of hollyhocks is rust, which shows up as small yellow or orange-brown powdery spots on the leaves. Cut off and discard any damaged foliage (or whole plants) at the first sign of attack. Avoid wetting foliage when watering, and water early in the day to allow plants to dry off before nightfall. While it won't eliminate present damage, a spray of sulfur will prevent future damage (see page 145).

Thrips

If there are silvery-white streaks on the foliage and the flower buds on your hollyhocks

Hollyhock, a biennial, has been a favorite for generations. Hollyhocks are now available in shades of pink, rose, red, purple, pale yellow, pale salmon, white and almost-black.

show brown edges or streaks and don't open properly, the problem is thrips. Two types—hollyhock thrips and gladiolus thrips—attack hollyhock flowers. Pick off and discard any damaged flowers, buds and foliage. Chemical controls include products that contain acephate, carbaryl or malathion (see pages 146-148). If thrips have previously been a problem, plant hollyhocks in another location the following year.

Two-Spotted Spider Mites

Unusually pale leaves, spotted with tiny white or yellow dots, sometimes with fine webbing, mean two-spotted spider mites have invaded your hollyhocks. Start control by knocking them off with a strong blast of water on the bottom of the leaves. Use an insecticidal soap or horticultural oil for additional control (see page 144). Chemical controls include miticides that contain the active ingredient hexakis (see page 148).

Hollyhocks are very easy to grow and often freely reseed themselves. Give them full sun and average soil and water and they'll take off—sometimes to a majestic height of 9 feet!

Anemone
JAPANESE OR CHINESE ANEMONES; WINDFLOWERS

Zones 6–10

Perennial

Black Blister Beetles

If an infestation of black blister beetles is present, you'll notice the small black or striped beetles, along with their damage—chewed anemone leaves and, if the infestation is heavy, complete defoliation of the plants. Black blister beetles present something of a dilemma for gardeners. While the adult beetles do some damage to anemones, the larvae of the beetles are excellent predators of a wide range of other plant-eating pests, including grasshoppers. Most gardeners put up with the relatively short-term damage from the beetles in exchange for the beneficial presence of their larvae.

Cutworms

If the new growth of your anemones is cut off right at soil level, you've probably got cutworms. Nocturnal feeders, these 1- to 2-inch-long worms can cause a lot of damage in just one night. If you've had problems with cutworms in the past, it's best to avoid their damage with preventative measures; one easy way is to make protective collars, as shown in the illustration on page 151, or apply Bt granules (see page 143) to the soil just as the new growth starts to appear. Chemical controls include carbaryl bait. Avoid problems in the future with an application of beneficial nematodes or parasitic wasps (see page 150).

Leafhoppers

If you notice small, distorted, yellowish leaves on your anemones, the problem is a virus-like culprit known as aster yellows. This malady is spread by aster leafhoppers (also known as the six-spotted leafhopper); to control it, you have to control the leafhoppers. Start by picking off any affected growth and disposing of it. The leafhoppers can be removed with a strong blast of water, or by using either an insecticidal soap or an application of light horticultural oil (see page 144); in any case, be sure to hit both the tops and bottoms of the leaves for complete control. If infestation continues, use an insecticide containing pyrethrum, azadirachtin or rotenone.

Chemical controls for leafhoppers include products containing acephate, carbaryl or

Japanese anemones do best in a semi-shaded location, with an evenly moist soil enriched with plenty of organic matter.

malathion (see pages 146-148). Make sure anemones are listed on the product label.

Rust

Powdery, reddish orange spores on anemone leaves indicate rust. With bad outbreaks of the disease, the plants will turn yellow, become stunted and probably won't bloom. Pick off and dispose of any infected leaves and immediately treat with a sulfur spray (see page 145). To avoid rust in the first place, avoid overhead watering, water early in the day so that foliage has a chance to dry off before nightfall, and keep plants well spaced to increase air circulation. If you use shears to cut off diseased foliage, sterilize them in rubbing alcohol after use so you don't spread the disease to other plants.

Slugs and Snails

If you wake up in the morning and find that something has eaten major portions of your anemone's new growth—something that has left a slime trail— you'll know the culprits are slugs, snails or both. Although there are a number of more-or-less effective natural controls, even the most ardent organic gardeners have begun using a product called Escar-Go, which contains iron phosphate, a naturally

occurring soil element (see page 145), to control these frustrating pests. Chemical controls include products (usually in bait form) containing metaldehyde or methiocarb (see page 148). Whether using Escar-Go or a chemical control, scatter it all around potential targets and

any damp, shady spot where slugs and snails hide during the day. If you know there are slugs or snails in your area, always treat your garden with a control before their damage is apparent; slugs and snails can do a tremendous amount of damage in even one night.

Valued for their late summer or early fall flowers, windflowers got their name because the tall, stiff stems sway in the wind, making the flowers look almost like butterflies.

Antirrhinum
SNAPDRAGON

Perennial, usually grown as an annual

All Zones

Today's snapdragons are available in a wide variety of forms, from 3-foot tall ones for the back of the flower border to dwarf forms no more than a few inches tall.

Aphids

Aphids, those masses of small tan, green or black insects, sometimes congregate on the new growth of snapdragons. Knock aphids off with a strong blast of water. If they persist, use an insecticidal soap or azadirachtin (see pages 142 and 144). Chemical controls include products that contain acephate, or malathion.

Leafrollers and Leaftiers

If you notice individual snapdragon leaves are folded or rolled, with or without fine webbing, the problem is leafrollers or leaftiers. If you unroll one of the leaves, you'll probably catch a small green, brown or yellow caterpillar in action. Pick off and discard any affected leaves. Control with sprays is difficult because the caterpillars are protected by the rolled or folded leaves. Chemical controls include products containing acephate or carbaryl (see page 146).

Rust

Rust is the most common disease to affect snapdragons. Pick off and discard any leaves showing powdery red spots. Water early in the day to allow foliage a chance to dry off before nightfall, and avoid overhead watering, which spreads the disease. As mentioned before, if rust is a problem (moist, cool weather encourages it), plant rust-resistant snapdragon varieties (see page 21). If the problem persists, use a sulfur spray, or fungicide containing chlorothalonil, mancozeb or myclobutanil (see pages 147-149).

If you've had a problem with rust on snapdragons in the past, use a fungicide to prevent this disease before it makes its first appearance, or plant disease-resistant varieties.

Artemisia
MUGWORT,
WORMWOOD

Zones 3–9

Woody perennials or shrubs

Aphids

If you notice colonies of small tan, green, yellow or dark-colored insects (along with their sticky residue) on the leaves of artemisia, you have an infestation of aphids. Aphids suck the sap from leaves and secrete a substance called honeydew, which in turn attracts ants and, eventually, a blackish mold called sooty mold. Blast aphids off plant leaves with a strong spray of water, or eliminate them by using an insecticidal soap (see page 144). Chemical controls for aphids on ornamental plants include products containing acephate (see page 146).

The true French tarragon, *Artemisia dranunculus*, is also a member of this family. As an edible herb, favor organic controls for aphids, or use a chemical control containing malathion or pyrethrins. Be sure to read and follow all label instructions, including the length of time to wait between spraying and harvesting the crop for culinary use.

Easy to grow and drought-resistant, the many varieties of artemisia are valued for their striking silver foliage. About the only thing they won't tolerate is too much shade and wet feet. Shown here: artemisia 'Silver Queen'.

Grasshoppers

Artemisia leaves eaten right down to the veins indicate the presence of those voracious eaters, grasshoppers. Only present during certain weather conditions—usually hot, dry weather—grasshoppers can do an amazing amount of damage quickly. If you've done a good job of attracting birds to your garden, they'll do an equally good job of controlling the grasshoppers. If the infestation gets out of control, spray with azadirachtin or use a chemical control containing acephate, carbaryl or malathion (see pages 146-148).

Rust

Rust shows up on artemisia leaves with orange-brown, powdery spots. The easiest control is to simply remove and dispose of any infected foliage and avoid overhead watering, which tends to spread the disease. If rust persists, use a fungicide containing triforine or chlorothalonil (see pages 147 and 149).

Garden designers love to combine the silver foliage of artemesias with white-, blue- and lavender-flowered plants. Shown here: A. stellerana, *commonly known as beach wormwood.*

Asclepias
BUTTERFLY WEED,
MILKWEED

Perennials or shrubs

Zones 3–9

Butterflies really do find the flowers of the butterfly weed irresistible. This perennial is about as hardy as they come, and can be planted virtually anywhere in the United States.

Leafminers

This plant is not bothered much by pests or diseases, but you may occasionally notice light brown trails in the leaves. These are the telltale marks of serpentine leafminers—tiny larvae that burrow inside the leaves. To control them, cut off and discard any affected foliage, then spray with an insecticide containing acephate or dimethoate (see pages 146-147). Prevent future infestations with a soil application of beneficial nematodes (see page 150).

Rust

Orange-brown, powdery spots on the foliage indicate rust. Damp weather and damp leaves encourage rust; control it by watering plants early in the day to allow foliage to dry off before nightfall. Avoid, if possible, any water on the foliage. Most attacks of rust on butterfly weed can be controlled by simply cutting off and discarding affected foliage, especially if you catch the disease early on.

Caterpillars

If you notice large, striped caterpillars munching their way through the foliage of your butterfly weed plants, it's best to simply let the caterpillars be. The eating period doesn't last long and these are the caterpillars which will soon transform themselves into monarch butterflies. Most gardeners simply look the other way during this feeding frenzy, or plant extra butterfly weed plants to satisfy the monarch caterpillar's appetite.

Butterfly weed does best in a full-sun location with only average soil, water and feeding. It actually prefers to be on the dry side during the summer months.

Aster
ASTER

Perennial

All Zones

Aphids

Small tan, green, yellow or dark-colored insects clustered together in colonies means you probably have aphids. They suck the sap from leaves and secrete sticky honeydew, which in turn attracts ants and a blackish mold. Aphids can be blasted off aster leaves with a strong spray of water, or eliminate them with an insecticidal soap (see page 144). Chemical controls for aphids on ornamental plants include products containing acephate (see page 146).

Asters do best in a full-sun location and will do fine with only average care; given evenly moist soil and once-a-month feedings, they'll really shine! Shown here: aster 'Patricia Ballard'.

Japanese Beetles

Most gardeners are familiar with the common Japanese beetle: $1/2$-inch-long, shiny green beetles which can devour leaves, flowers and buds with amazing speed. Most prevalent from June through October, especially during periods of warm weather; control Japanese beetles with azadirachtin, beneficial nematodes and milky disease spores. All destroy the soil-borne grubs before they become a problem (see page 150). You can also control the beetles with insecticides containing rotenone or pyrethrum. Chemical controls include products containing acephate, carbaryl or malathion (see pages 146 and 148).

Lacebugs

Aster leaves speckled with yellow, gray, white or green spots may indicate the presence of chrysanthemum lacebugs. You'll know for sure if you turn the affected leaves over and notice telltale shiny black droppings on the leaves' undersides. Control lacebugs with insecticidal soap or horticultural oil (see page 144), with special attention to the undersides of leaves. Chemical controls include products containing acephate (see page 146).

Small, wedge-shaped leafhoppers do exactly what their name suggests: hop into the air when the foliage they have infected is disturbed. Leafhoppers don't do much physical damage, but are carriers of diseases which can cause serious problems for asters.

Leafhoppers

If the leaves of your asters look bleached or stippled, have yellow or brown edges, or are deformed, the culprits are probably aster leafhoppers (also known as six-spotted leafhoppers). The leafhoppers suck the sap from the bottoms of aster foliage and, in the process, infect the plants with a disease known as aster yellows. Control aster leafhoppers with insecticidal soap or horticultural oil (see page 144), paying close attention to the undersides of leaves. Chemical controls include products containing acephate, carbaryl or malathion (see pages 146-148).

Leaf Spot

Leaf spot (leaf blight) shows up as transparent black or brown spots on aster leaves. The spots enlarge over time. Wet weather increases the chances of leaf spot. Cut off any infected foliage (or entire plants) and discard as soon as the disease appears. Control with a fungicide containing chlorothalonil, mancozeb or zineb (see pages 147-148).

Powdery Mildew

Aster leaves, stems or flowers covered with a grayish white powder is a sure sign of the disease known as powdery mildew. Damp, cool weather encourages powdery mildew, as do shady growing conditions. If powdery mildew has been a problem before, be sure and favor mildew-resistant aster varieties such as *Aster* x *frikartii* and 'Wood's Pink'; avoid types particularly susceptible to mildew such as *A. novae-angliae* and *A. novi-belgii*. Cut off any damaged foliage (or whole plants) and discard. Although existing damage cannot be eliminated, prevent future outbreaks of powdery mildew with a sulfur spray (see page 145).

Rust

Rust causes aster leaves to turn yellow and show powdery orange-brown spots. Spread by the wind, rust is best controled by removing any infected foliage (or whole plants) as soon as the disease makes an appearance. To prevent further problems, spray plants with a liquid sulfur or baking soda spray (see pages 143 and 145).

Aster frikartii is one of the best of all asters for home gardens. It blooms over a very long season, with plenty of lavender to almost-violet flowers.

Astilbe
FALSE SPIRAEA,
MEADOW SWEET

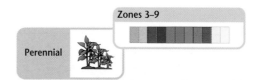

Perennial Zones 3–9

Aphids

If new growth is stunted or deformed and you notice colonies of small green, yellow, brown or black insects, you've probably got aphids. Aphids suck the sap from leaves and secrete a sticky substance called honeydew, which in turn attracts ants and, eventually, the blackish sooty mold. Aphids can be blasted off astilbe leaves with a strong spray of water, or eliminated by use of an insecticidal soap or horticultural oil (see page 144). Chemical controls for aphids on ornamental plants include products containing acephate (see page 146).

Black Vine Weevils

If the edges of astilbe foliage are eaten away, the problem is likely to be black vine weevils. One of the most effective controls is an application of beneficial nematodes (see page 150). For complete control, two applications (one in the spring and one in late summer) may be necessary. Chemical controls include products containing acephate (see page 146).

Fusarium Wilt

Fusarium wilt is a frustrating soil-borne disease that causes astilbe plants to turn yellow, or individual leaves to turn brown, eventually killing the plant. To avoid the problem, incorporate plenty of leafmold or peat moss into the soil to improve soil drainage. If fusarium wilt attacks, completely remove and discard the affected plant, along with any soil the roots have come in contact with. If fusarium wilt has previously been a problem, plant astilbes in another location.

Astilbes accept a variety of garden locations, from full sun to partial shade. They do best in an evenly moist, well-drained soil, amended with plenty of organic matter.

Japanese Beetles

Those small, green pests known as Japanese beetles will occasionally attack astilbe foliage, eating holes in young leaves and flower buds. Most prevalent from June through October, especially during periods of warm weather, Japanese beetles can be controlled with azadirachtin, beneficial nematodes and milky spores, which destroy the soil-borne grubs before they become a problem (see page 150). Chemical controls include products containing acephate, carbaryl or malathion (see pages 146 and 148).

Powdery Mildew

Astilbe foliage which is covered with a powdery white substance indicates the presence of the disease known as powdery mildew. While it doesn't kill the plants, it can render them so unattractive that gardeners wish the plants would die. To begin control, cut off and discard any affected foliage. Although existing damage cannot be eliminated, future outbreaks of powdery mildew can be prevented with a spray of liquid sulfur or baking soda (see pages 143 and 145).

Slugs and Snails

Slugs and snails can completely devour plants overnight, especially when the tender new astilbe shoots are just emerging from the soil. Although there are a number of more-or-less effective natural controls, even the most ardent organic gardeners have begun using a product called Escar-Go (which contains iron phosphate, a naturally occurring soil element—see page 145), to control these frustrating pests. Chemical controls include products (usually in bait form) containing metaldehyde or methiocarb (see page 148). Whether using Escar-Go or a chemical control, scatter it all around potential targets and any damp, shady spot where slugs and snails hide during the day. If you know there are slugs or snails in your area, always treat your garden with a control before their damage is apparent; slugs and snails can do a tremendous amount of damage in even one night.

With their feathery, plume-like flowers, available in shades of pink, rose, red and white, astilbes are one of the few perennials willing to bloom in the shade. Shown here: astilbe 'Meadow Sweet'.

Begonia
BEGONIA

Annuals   All Zones

Aphids

Aphids cluster in colonies, especially on new growth, and these small insects range in color from tan to green to brownish black. They secrete a sticky substance known as honeydew which, in turn, attracts ants and eventually a dark, sooty mold. Avoid all these symptoms by getting rid of the aphids at the first sign of attack. To begin control, knock the aphids off the foliage with a strong blast of water. If they persist, use an insecticidal soap (see page 144). Chemical controls include products containing acephate or malathion (see pages 146-148).

Bacterial Leaf Spot

Bacterial leaf spot starts as small translucent spots on leaves. The spots gradually enlarge and turn the leaf brown with yellow edges; over time the affected leaves fall off. Leaf spot is spread by water—either rain or from the garden hose—and is most likely to be a problem during wet spring weather. Remove and discard any damaged leaves (or entire plants) at the first sign of attack. Keep the disease from spreading by watering early in the day to allow foliage a chance to dry off before nightfall; avoid overhead watering. Chemical controls include products containing copper sulfate or streptomycin (see page 143). After pruning affected foliage, dip shears in rubbing alcohol to avoid transmitting the disease to healthy plants.

Black Vine Weevils

Black vine weevils—small, dark beetles—will occasionally attack begonias, eating a scallop-pattern around the edges of leaves during the night. To control, apply beneficial nematodes in the spring and again in late summer (see page 150). Knockdown chemical controls include products containing acephate (see page 146).

Mass planted, wax begonias make quite a statement and bloom over a very long season. Shown here: 'Ambassador'.

Viewed up close, the flowers of wax begonias have an iridescence that makes them look almost like jewels. Shown here: a begonia in the Cocktail series known as 'Gin'.

Mealybugs

You'll definitely know if your begonias have mealybugs: Their distinctive fuzzy white bodies (about $1/4$ inch long) look like nothing else in the pest world. If you notice mealybugs on the foliage, start control by knocking them off with a strong blast of water. If the problem persists, spray with an insecticidal soap, paying special attention to the undersides of leaves (see page 144), or an insecticide containing azadirachtin or pyrethrum. Chemical controls include products containing acephate, malathion or carbaryl (see pages 146-148).

Root Rot

If you notice the base of your begonia plants rotting and turning black, the problem is root rot. Dig up and discard infected plants at the first sign of attack. Avoid the problem by planting begonias in a very well drained soil, amended with plenty of compost, leafmold or peat moss.

Slugs and Snails

Slugs and snails can do an immense amount of damage. You'll notice leaves or entire plants ravaged, along with the telltale slimy, shiny trails of slugs and snails. Although there are a number of more-or-less effective natural controls, even the most ardent organic gardeners have begun using a product called Escar-Go (which contains iron phosphate, a naturally occurring soil element—see page 145), to control these frustrating pests. Chemical controls include products (usually in bait form) containing metaldehyde or methiocarb (see page 148). Whether using Escar-Go or a chemical control, scatter it all around potential targets and any damp, shady spot where slugs and snails hide during the day. If you know there are slugs or snails in your area, always treat your garden with a control before their damage is broad.

Spring Dwarf Nematodes

Spring dwarf nematodes feed inside begonia leaves, turning the leaves brown, starting at the bottom and moving to the top. These unusual pests cause additional problems that are sometimes confused with disease: yellow, distorted foliage and stunted plants. Dig up and discard infected plants at the first sign of attack.

Thrips

The damage from these tiny insects shows up as silvery streaking on leaves and as distorted new growth. Begin control by knocking thrips off foliage with a strong blast of water. If the problem persists, use an insecticidal soap or azadirachtin (see pages 142 and 144). Chemical controls include products containing acephate or malathion (see pages 146-148).

Whiteflies

If you brush past a begonia plant and you notice clouds of small white insects flying up, you have an infestation of whiteflies. These pesky insects can be controlled with insecticidal soap or azadirachtin (see pages 142 and 144). Chemical controls include products containing malathion or carbaryl (see pages 146-148).

Annual begonias do best in a lightly shaded location with evenly moist soil, amended with plenty of organic matter and once-a-month applications of fertilizer.

Calendula
POT MARIGOLD

Annual All Zones

Aphids

Aphids cluster in colonies, especially on new growth. These small insects range in color from tan to green, to brownish black and secrete sticky honeydew which, in turn, attracts ants and eventually sooty mold. Avoid all these symptoms by getting rid of the aphids at the first sign of attack: Knock the aphids off the foliage with a strong blast of water. If they persist, use an insecticidal soap (see page 144). Chemical controls include products containing acephate or malathion (see pages 146-148).

Cercospora Leaf Spot

Different-sized spots on calendula leaves (in shades of brown, black, purple or yellow) are a sure sign of leaf spot. Best bet is to completely remove and destroy any affected plants at the first sign of attack. Avoid the problem by watering plants early in the day to allow foliage to dry before evening, and avoid wetting the foliage. If you use pruning shears to remove diseased foliage, dip the blades in rubbing alcohol before reuse.

Powdery Mildew

Calendula foliage that is covered with a powdery white substance is suffering from powdery mildew. While it doesn't kill the plants, it can render them so unattractive that gardeners wish the plants would die. Begin control by

cutting off and discarding any affected foliage. Although existing damage cannot be eliminated, future outbreaks of powdery mildew can be prevented with a spray of liquid sulfur or baking soda (see pages 143 and 145).

Slugs and Snails

Slugs and snails can do an immense amount of damage quickly. You'll notice leaves or entire plants ravaged and eaten, along with the telltale sign of slugs and snails—slimy, shiny trails. Although there are a number of more-or-less effective controls, even the most ardent organic gardeners have begun using Escar-Go (which contains iron phosphate, a naturally occurring soil element—see page 145), to control these frustrating pests. Chemical controls include products (usually in

bait form) containing metaldehyde or methiocarb (see page 148). Whether using Escar-Go or a chemical control, scatter it all around potential targets and any damp, shady spot where slugs and snails hide during the day. If you know there are slugs or snails in your area, always treat your garden with a control before their damage is apparent, especially right after putting out new transplants.

Whiteflies

If you brush past a calendula plant and you notice clouds of small white insects flying up, you have whiteflies. These pesky insects can be controlled with insecticidal soap or azadirachtin (see pages 142 and 144). Chemical controls include products containing malathion or carbaryl (see pages 146-148).

Calendulas are one of the first annuals to put on a really big show, preferring the cooler weather of late winter and early spring. Plant in a full-sun location with a well-drained soil and you'll succeed with this cheerful performer.

Canna
CANNA

Tender perennial, grown from a rhizome

Zones 8–10

Canna Bud Rot

Canna bud rot shows up as dark streaks in canna leaves. It is caused by harmful soil-borne bacteria. If this disease shows up, immediately dig up and discard any affected plants. About the only prevention is to grow cannas in very well drained soil.

Japanese Beetles

If you see small holes eaten right through canna leaves the culprit is likely to be Japanese beetles. The beetles are metallic green or brownish and about $1/2$ inch long. Control with insecticidal soap (see page 144). Control future generations with milky spores, which kill the grubs as they overwinter in the soil (see page 150). Chemical controls include products that contain acephate, carbaryl or malathion (see pages 146-148).

Leafrollers

Damaged canna leaves, some of which may be rolled or held together with fine webbing, indicate the presence of leafrollers. There are two different caterpillars, between one and two inches long, which prey on cannas. About the only control is to cut off and discard any damaged leaves at the first sign of attack.

Spotted Cucumber Beetles

Spotted cucumber beetles munch on canna leaves and flowers, leaving holes or ragged edges. The beetles themselves are about $1/4$ inch long, yellowish green in color, with black spots. Beneficial nematodes will help prevent spotted cucumber beetles (see page 150). Chemical controls include products that contain carbaryl or pyrethrins (see pages 146-149).

With their dramatic foliage and flowers, cannas are sure to call attention to themselves. They do best in a full-sun location with average soil, water and feeding. That said, cannas are one of the few flowering plants that actually do well in very wet soil, such as next to a pond or pool.

Celosia
COCKSCOMB

Annual · All Zones

Leaf Spot

Different-sized spots on *Celosia* leaves, in shades of brown, black, purple or yellow, are a sure sign of leaf spot. Cut off and discard any damaged foliage (or whole plants) as soon as possible. Water plants early in the day so foliage dries before evening, and avoid wetting the foliage. If you use pruning shears to remove diseased foliage, clean the blades in rubbing alcohol before reuse.

Spider Mites

Spider mites can attack *Celosia*, especially during periods of hot, dry weather. Telltale damage includes stippled, grayish foliage and stunted growth. The mites attack the undersides of leaves and usually leave small holes and fine webbing in their wake. Blast mites off with a strong spray of water, paying particular attention to the undersides of the leaves. If the problem persists, use an insecticidal soap (see page 144) specially formulated for controlling mites.

Celosias— particularly the crested type shown here—produce some of the most unusual flowers of any annual. Plant in full sun and provide average soil, water and feedings.

Southern Root-Knot Nematodes

Southern root-knot nematodes—microscopic, soil-borne worms—cause stunted growth and yellow foliage. Affected plants eventually die. If you pull up a plant, you'll notice stunted roots with small knots or lumps on them. Dig up and destroy any affected plants. To avoid the problem in the future, solarize the soil (see page 151) and incorporate plenty of organic soil amendments into the planting bed. The product Nematrol has shown some success in controlling southern root-knot nematodes, as does incorporating chitin into the soil (see page 143).

The plume-type celosias produce some of the most brilliantly colored—almost fluorescent—flowers imaginable.

Centaurea
BACHELOR'S BUTTONS, CORNFLOWER

Annuals and perennials

Annuals: All Zones

Perennials: Zones 3–10

Aphids

Aphids cluster in colonies, especially on new growth. These small insects range in color from tan to green, to brownish black and the sticky substance they secrete, known as honeydew, in turn attracts ants and eventually a dark, sooty mold. Avoid all these symptoms by getting rid of the aphids at the first sign of attack. Knock the aphids off the foliage with a strong blast of water. If they persist, use an insecticidal soap (see page 144). Chemical controls include products containing acephate or malathion (see pages 146-148).

Aster Yellows

Aster yellows shows up in gardens as the weather warms. Symptoms of this problem include distorted new growth, brown edges on older leaves, distorted or nonexistent flowers, or flowers which remain green. Affected plants should be dug up and destroyed at the first sign of attack. Leafhopper insects spread this disease from plant to plant. Control leafhoppers with pyrethrin, azadirachtin, rotenone, or an insecticide containing malathion or carbaryl.

Cutworms

Cutworms, the soil-borne larvae of a variety of moth, are the bane of many gardeners. Particularly frustrating is that cutworms prefer newly planted transplants and seedlings, cutting them off right at the base. The best mechanical control is to form a paper collar (or cut off the bottom of a paper cup, or remove the top and bottom of an aluminum can) and place it as protection around the plant. Introduce cutworm predators into the garden, such as beneficial soil nematodes, parasitoid wasps and tachinid flies (see page 150).

Downy Mildew

Downy mildew is a disease prevalent in damp, cool weather. It shows up as a powdery, white coating on leaves. Remove any affected foliage or completely dig up and destroy any diseased plants at the first sign of attack. To avoid the problem, water plants early in the day so foliage has a chance to dry off before nightfall; space plants widely for increased air circulation. No fungicide will cure existing disease, but it may prevent future infection. Spray with a product containing maneb or chlorothalonil.

Loved for their true blue flowers, bachelor's buttons do best in a full-sun location with average water, soil and feedings. About the only thing they won't tolerate is an acid soil; add lime if your soil is on the acidic side.

Bachelor's buttons come in a variety of colors, from deep to pale blue, shades of pink and rose, and white.

Hemispherical Scale

Hemispherical scale looks like brownish bumps on the stems of plants. The tough outer coating on scale protects the small insect inside, which damages the plant by sucking juices from the stem. If the infestation is not large, simply scrape the scale off the plant using the edge of a dull knife or a plastic scouring pad. Avoid problems with scale by attracting such natural predators as lacewing larvae and beneficial wasps. Horticultural oils will smother the insects inside their protective coatings; use a light horticultural oil during the summer or a dormant oil while the plant is dormant (with annual flowers, this is obviously not an option). Chemical controls include products containing dimethoate or acephate.

Leafhoppers

If you notice small, distorted, yellowish leaves on your bachelor's buttons, the problem is a virus-like culprit known as aster yellows. The disease is spread by aster leafhoppers (also known as the six-spotted leafhopper). To control the disease, you have to control the leafhoppers. Start by picking off any affected growth and disposing of it. Remove the leafhoppers with a strong blast of water, or use an insecticidal soap (see page 144); in either case, be sure to hit both the tops and bottoms of the leaves for complete control. Chemical controls for leafhoppers include products containing acephate, carbaryl or malathion (see pages 146-148).

Omnivorous Leaftiers

If you notice individual folded or rolled leaves, with or without fine webbing, the problem is leafrollers or leaftiers. If you unroll one of the leaves, you'll probably catch one of the culprits in action: small green, brown or yellow caterpillars. Pick off and discard any affected leaves. Control is difficult because the rolled or folded leaves protect the caterpillars. When you first notice damage, use either a spray of Bt or a chemical insecticide containing acephate or carbaryl (see page 146).

Powdery Mildew

Bachelors' buttons foliage covered with a powdery white substance indicates the presence of powdery mildew. While this disease doesn't kill the plants, it can render them so unattractive you wish they would die. Begin control by cutting off and discarding any affected foliage. Although existing damage cannot be eliminated, future outbreaks of powdery mildew can be prevented with a sulfur spray (see page 145).

Rust

Orange-brown, powdery spots on the foliage indicate the presence of the disease known as rust. Rust is encouraged by damp weather and damp leaves. Control rust by watering plants early in the day to allow foliage to dry off before nightfall, and avoid, if possible, any water on the foliage. Most attacks of rust on bachelor's buttons can be controlled by simply cutting off and discarding affected foliage, especially if you catch the disease early on.

Southern Blight

Southern blight is a problem for bachelor's buttons planted in warm climates. The foliage turns yellow, wilts, and whole plants may rot at the base and strange webbing or fungus strings form on the soil in the presence of this disease. To avoid this problem, plant bachelor's buttons in well-drained soil and then allow the soil to dry out between waterings. Pull up and discard any affected plants at the first sign of attack. Remove the infected soil 6 inches beyond the root ball. If you want to replant the area with susceptible plants, solarize the soil (see page 151) for 4 to 6 weeks before planting.

Chrysanthemum
CHRYSANTHEMUM

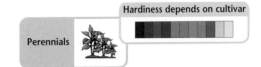

Perennials

Hardiness depends on cultivar

The stars of the fall garden, chrysanthemums require only a full-sun location, good garden loam, regular watering and once-a-month feedings to put on a vibrant show.

ing foliage affected with aster yellows, because the virus-like disease can be spread by simply touching leaves and flowers of healthy plants. If you use pruning shears to cut out affected foliage, disinfect the blades in rubbing alcohol.

Botrytis Blight

Botrytis blight is also known as gray mold. Symptoms include drooping flowers which then turn brown and become covered with a gray, fuzzy mold. Dig up and destroy any infected plants at the first sign of attack. Avoid the problem by avoiding overhead watering, making sure the soil has excellent drainage; also space plants far apart to improve air circulation. Existing disease cannot be cured, but you can prevent future outbreaks with a fungicide containing chlorothalonil (see page 147).

Lacebugs

Chrysanthemum leaves speckled with yellow, gray, white or green spots may indicate the presence of chrysanthemum lacebugs. You'll know for sure if you turn the affected leaves over and notice telltale shiny black droppings on the undersides of the leaves. Control lacebugs with insecticidal soap or horticultural oil (see page 144), with special attention to the undersides of leaves. Chemical controls include products containing acephate (see page 146).

Leafminers

Light brown trails in chrysanthemum leaves are the telltale marks of serpentine leafminers—tiny larvae burrowing inside the leaves. To control, cut off and discard any affected foliage. Prevent future infestations with a soil applica-

Aphids

Aphids, those masses of small tan, green or black insects, sometimes congregate on the new growth of chrysanthemums. To start control, knock aphids off with a strong blast of water. If they persist, use an insecticidal soap or azadirachtin (see pages 142 and 144). Chemical controls include products which contain acephate or malathion (see pages 146-148).

Aster Yellows

Weakened leaves and a mottled yellow appearance indicate this disease. Since there is no cure for aster yellows, simply remove and destroy any affected plants. Wash hands with soap and hot water after touch-

tion of beneficial nematodes (see page 150).

Leaf Spot

Different-sized spots on chrysanthemum leaves, in shades of brown, black, purple or yellow are a sure sign of leaf spot. Cut off and discard any damaged foliage (or whole plants) as soon as possible. Water plants early in the day so foliage dries before evening, and avoid wetting the foliage. If you use pruning shears to remove diseased foliage, dip the blades in rubbing alcohol before reuse, to disinfect them.

Powdery Mildew

Chrysanthemum foliage covered with a powdery white substance indicates the disease powdery mildew. It doesn't kill the plants, but makes them quite unattractive. Begin control by cutting off and discarding any affected foliage. Although existing damage cannot be eliminated, prevent future outbreaks of powdery mildew with a sulfur spray (see page 145).

Ray Blight

Ray blight is a disease which causes much disappointment for chrysanthemum growers. Symptoms include flower buds that turn black and fail to open, or fully open flowers that die. Dig up and destroy any infected plants at the first sign of attack. Here's how to avoid the problem in the future: Space plants generously to increase air circulation and to keep water off the foliage.

Rust

Orange-brown, powdery spots on the foliage indicate the presence of the disease known as rust. Rust is encouraged by damp weather and damp leaves, so you can help control it by watering plants early in the day to allow foliage to dry off before nightfall; avoid, if possible, any water on the foliage. Most attacks of rust on chrysanthemums can be controlled by simply cutting off and discarding affected foliage, especially if you catch the disease early on.

Thrips

The damage from these tiny insects shows up as silvery streaking on leaves and as distorted new growth. Knock thrips off foliage with a strong blast of water. If

the problem persists, use an insecticidal soap or azadirachtin (see pages 142 and 144). Chemical controls include products containing acephate, carbaryl or malathion(see pages 146-148).

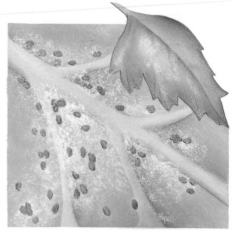

Two-spotted spider mites sometimes infest chrysanthemums, leaving behind pale foliage and their characteristic fine webbing. You can control these pesky mites with insecticidal soap.

Two-Spotted Spider Mites

Unusually pale leaves, spotted with tiny white or yellow dots, sometimes with fine webbing, mean two-spotted spider mites have invaded your chrysanthemums. Start control by knocking them off with a strong blast of water. Use an insecticidal soap for additional control (see page 144). Chemical controls include miticides which include the active ingredient hexakis (see page 148).

Viruses

If your chrysanthemum plants are stunted with mottled, streaked or unusually colored foliage, the problem is a virus. Since there is no known cure for viral diseases, dig up and destroy any infected plants at the first sign of attack.

Mimicking autumn's foliage colors, chrysanthemums come in a wonderful range of colors from rust red to orange, yellow, pink and white.

Cleome
SPIDER FLOWER

All Zones

Perennial, grown as an annual

Aphids

Aphids cluster in colonies, especially on new growth. These small insects range in color from tan to green, to brownish black and secrete a sticky substance known as honeydew. The honeydew, in turn, attracts ants and eventually a dark, sooty mold. To avoid all these symptoms, get rid of the aphids at the first sign of attack by knocking them off the foliage with a strong blast of water. If they persist, use an insecticidal soap (see page 144). Chemical controls include products containing acephate or malathion (see pages 146-148).

Leaf Spot

Different-sized spots on cleome leaves, in shades of brown, black, purple or yellow, are a sure sign of leaf spot. Cut off and discard any damaged foliage (or whole plants) as soon as possible. Water plants early in the day to allow foliage to dry before evening, and don't wet the foliage. If you use pruning

Reaching 4 to 6 feet tall and almost as wide, cleome is one of the easiest flowers to grow. Give them a full-sun location and average soil, water and fertilizer, and stand back! They'll take off and provide beautiful flowers in shades of rose, red, pink and white all summer long.

shears to remove diseased foliage, dip the blades in rubbing alcohol afterward to disinfect.

Coleus
COLEUS

All Zones

Perennial, grown as an annual

With their fantastically patterned leaves and brilliant colors, coleus lend a tropical look to any garden. Coleus prefer a location with light shade and rich, evenly moist soil. Feed once a month .

Mealybugs

You'll definitely know if your coleus have mealybugs: The mealybugs' distinctive fuzzy-white bodies (about $1/4$ inch long) look like nothing else in the pest world. If you notice mealybugs on the foliage, start control by knocking them off with a strong blast of water. If the infestation continues, spray with an insecticidal soap, paying special attention to the undersides of leaves (see page 144). Chemical controls include products containing malathion or carbaryl or (see pages 146-148).

Southern Root-Knot Nematodes

Southern root-knot nematodes—microscopic, soil-borne worms—cause stunted growth and yellow foliage. Affected plants eventually die. If you pull up a plant, you'll notice stunted roots

with small knots or lumps on them. Dig up and destroy any affected plants. Solarize the soil (see page 151) and incorporate plenty of organic soil amendments into the planting bed, to prevent future problems. The product Nematrol has shown some success in controlling southern root-knot nematodes, as does incorporating chitin into the soil (see page 143).

Whiteflies

If clouds of small white insects fly up from your coleus, you have an infestation of whiteflies. Control these pesky insects with insecticidal soap or azadirachtin (see pages 142 and 144). Chemical controls include products containing malathion or carbaryl (see pages 146-148).

Convallaria
LILY-OF-THE-VALLEY

Perennial, grown from a small rhizome

Zones 2–9

With its small, fragrant, bell-shaped flowers, lily-of-the-valley has been a garden fa-vorite for generations. Lily-of-the-valley prefer a partially shaded location and aver-age garden soil, water and feedings. In most locations, lily-of-the-valley are very long-lived and will spread to cover a wide area.

For such a delicate looking flower, lilies-of-the-valley are surprisingly sturdy—and wonderfully fragrant!

Slugs and Snails

Slugs and snails can do a lot of damage in a short period of time. Leaves or entire plants may be ravaged and eaten, and you'll see the telltale sign of slugs and snails—slimy, shiny trails. Although there are a number of natural controls, even the most ardent organic gardeners use a product called Escar-Go (which contains iron phosphate, a naturally occur-ring soil element—see page 145), to control these slugs and snails. Chemical controls in-clude products (usually in bait form) containing metaldehyde or methiocarb (see page 148). Whether using Escar-Go or a chemical control, scatter it all around potential targets and any damp, shady spot where slugs and snails hide during the day. If you know there are slugs or snails in your area, always treat your garden with a control before their damage is apparent, especially right after putting out new transplants.

Southern Blight

Southern blight is a problem for lily-of-the-valley planted in warm climates. Whole plants rot at the base and strange webbing or fungus strings form on the soil in the presence of this disease. How to avoid? Plant lily-of-the-valley in well-drained soil and then allow the soil to dry out between water-ings. Pull up and discard any af-fected plants at the first sign of attack. Avoid future problems by solarizing the soil (see page 151).

Cosmos
COSMOS

Annual   All Zones

Aphids

If you notice colonies of small tan, green, yellow or dark-colored insects (along with their sticky residue) on the leaves of cosmos, you have an infestation of aphids. Aphids suck the sap from leaves and leave behind a sticky substance, called honeydew, which in turn attracts ants and eventually a blackish mold. Aphids can be blasted off plant leaves with a strong spray of water, or eliminated by use of an insecticidal soap (see page 144). Chemical controls for aphids on ornamental plants include products containing acephate (see page 146).

Aster Yellows

Aster yellows weaken foliage and give it a mottled yellow appearance. Since there is no cure for this disease, simply remove and destroy any affected plants. Wash hands with soap

Related to Cosmos bipinnatus, Cosmos sulphureus *is available in a completely different range of warm colors. Shown here is cosmos 'Sunny Red'.*

and hot water after touching foliage affected with aster yellows, because the virus can be spread to healthy plants easily. If you use pruning shears to cut out affected foliage, disinfect the blades in rubbing alcohol after use.

Japanese Beetles

Most gardeners are familiar with the common Japanese beetle: $1/2$-inch-long, shiny green beetles which can devour leaves, flowers and buds with amazing speed. Most prevalent from June through October, especially during periods of warm weather, you can control Japanese beetles with azadirachtin, beneficial nematodes and milky disease spores, all of which destroy the soil-borne grubs before they become a problem (see page 150). Chemical controls include products containing acephate, carbaryl, or malathion (see pages 146 and 148).

Spider Mites

Spider mites often attack plants stressed by lack of water. Leaves will appear speckled, along with minute webbing; affected foliage will eventually turn yellow and drop. Avoid spider mites by keeping plants well watered. Control by spraying infested foliage with a strong blast of water. If the problem persists, spray

with insecticidal soap or light horticultural oil (see page 144).

Spotted Cucumber Beetles

Spotted cucumber beetles munch on cosmos leaves and flowers, leaving holes or ragged edges. The beetles themselves are about $1/4$ inch long, yellowish green in color, with black spots. Beneficial nematodes will help prevent spotted cucumber beetles (see page 150). Chemical controls include products which contain carbaryl or pyrethrins (see pages 146-149).

One of the best annuals for cut flowers, cosmos need a full-sun location, along with average soil, water and feedings.

Cosmos bipinnatus *is available in shades of pink, rose and white.*

Delphinium
DELPHINIUM

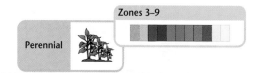

Perennial

Zones 3–9

For flowers like these, plant delphiniums in a full-sun location with rich soil. Provide regular watering and once-a-month feedings.

Aphids

Aphids—masses of small tan, green or black insects—sometimes congregate on the new growth of delphinium. First, knock aphids off with a strong blast of water. If they persist, use an insecticidal soap or azadirachtin (see pages 142 and 144). Chemical controls include products that contain acephate or malathion (see pages 146-148).

Bacterial Leaf Spot

Bacterial leaf spot starts as small translucent spots on leaves. The spots gradually enlarge and turn brown with yellow edges, and over time the affected leaves turn yellow and fall off. Leaf spot is spread by water—either rain or from the garden hose—and is most likely to be a problem during wet spring weather. Remove and discard any damaged leaves (or entire plants) at the first sign of attack. Keep disease from spreading: water early in the day to allow foliage a chance to dry off before nightfall; avoid overhead watering. Chemical controls include products containing copper sulfate or streptomycin (see page 143). After pruning affected foliage, disinfect the shears in rubbing alcohol to avoid transmitting the disease to healthy plants.

One of the best ways to avoid problems with diseases like bacterial leaf spot: Avoid wetting delphinium foliage. Water early in the morning so foliage has a chance to dry off before nightfall.

One of the most spectacular of all flowering plants, dephiniums may need a little help in the form of staking to help keep their magnificient heads up high.

Common Stalk Borers

Common stalk borers are brown, $3/4$- to $1^1/2$-inch-long caterpillars that bore holes right in the stems of plants and live inside, eating the plants from the inside out. If sections of plants suddenly wilt, despite sufficient water, check for telltale small holes in the stems surrounded by a fine sawdust-like material called frass. Dig up and destroy any infected plants, or portions of plants. These damaging caterpillars can be controlled with a spray of Bt (see page 143).

Cyclamen Mites

Cyclamen mites are very small insects prevalent during periods of cool weather. Affected plants will be stunted and deformed; flowers may turn black. There's not much you can do about these pests except to dig up and destroy any infected plants at the first sign of attack.

Larkspur Leafminers

Larkspur leafminers are the very small larvae of a tiny fly. The larvae mine their way into the leaves, producing characteristic serpentine, tan-colored trails on the foliage. Prune off and destroy any affected foliage. To avoid future problems with leafminers, apply beneficial nematodes to the soil (see page 150).

Slugs and Snails

Slugs and snails can completely devour plants overnight, especially tender new growth. Although there are a number of more-or-less effective natural controls, a product called Escar-Go (which contains iron phosphate, a naturally occurring soil element—see page 145), controls these frustrating pests fairly gently. Chemical controls include products (usually in bait form) containing metaldehyde or methiocarb (see page 148). Whether using Escar-Go or a chemical control, scatter it all around potential targets and any damp, shady spot where slugs and snails hide during the day. If you know there are slugs or snails in your area, always treat your garden with a control before their damage is apparent; slugs and snails can wreak havoc, in even one night.

Spider Mites

Spider mites can attack delphinium, especially during periods of hot, dry weather. Telltale damage includes stippled, grayish foliage and stunted growth. The mites attack the undersides of leaves and usually leave small holes and fine webbing in their wake. Blast mites off with a strong spray of water, paying particular attention to the undersides of the leaves. If the problem persists, use an insecticidal soap (see page 144) specially formulated for controlling mites.

Available in a variety of blue and lavender shades, with contrasting "eyes" in white and black, delphinium can become the focal point of any garden.

Dianthus
COTTAGE PINKS,
BORDER CARNATIONS

Perennials and annuals, depending on species

Zones 3–9

Bacterial Leaf Spot

Bacterial leaf spot starts as small translucent spots on leaves which gradually enlarge and turn brown with yellow edges; over time the affected leaves turn yellow and fall off. Water—either rain or from the garden hose—spreads leaf spot, and is most likely to be a problem during wet spring weather.

Pinks and carnations of been favorites of home gardeners for generations. Loved for their intricately patterned flowers— not to mention their haunting fragrance—plant them in a full sun location and in rich garden loam. Provide regular watering and feeding.

Remove and discard any damaged leaves (or entire plants) at the first sign of attack. To keep disease from spreading, water early in the day to allow foliage a chance to dry off before nightfall; avoid overhead watering. Chemical controls include products containing copper sulfate or streptomycin (see page 143). After pruning affected foliage, dip shears in rubbing alcohol to avoid transmitting the disease to healthy plants.

Cutworms

If the new growth of your dianthus plants is cut off right at soil level, you've probably got cutworms. These 1- to 2-inch-long nocturnal feeders can cause a lot of damage in just one night. It's best to avoid cutworm damage with preventative measures; one easy way is to make protective collars (see page 151) or apply Bt granules (see page 143) to the soil just as the new growth starts to appear. Chemical controls include products with the active ingredient acephate (see page 146).

Rust

If dianthus foliage turns yellow and shows powdery orange-brown spots, the plants have become infected with rust, spread by the wind. The best control for this disease is to remove any infected foliage (or whole plants) as soon as the rust makes an appearance. To prevent further problems, spray plants with a sulfur solution (see page 145).

Spider Mites

Spider mites can attack dianthus, especially during periods of hot, dry weather. Stippled, grayish foliage and stunted growth are the telltale damage. The mites attack the undersides of leaves and usually leave small holes and fine webbing in their wake. Blast mites off with a strong spray of water; pay particular attention to the undersides of the leaves. If the problem persists, use an insecticidal soap (see page 144) specially formulated for the control of mites.

Viruses

If your dianthus plants or flowers are stunted with mottled, streaked or unusually colored foliage, the problem is a virus. Since there is no cure for viral diseases, dig up and destroy any infected plants at the first sign of attack. Help avoid viruses or viral diseases by controlling insects, such as aphids and leafhoppers, which spread viruses as they suck on plants. A spray of insecticidal soap will control both aphids and leafhoppers (see page 144).

Dicentra
BLEEDING HEART

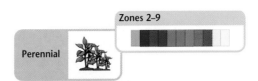

Perennial

Zones 2–9

It's hard to resist the charms of bleeding heart, with its arching stems and heart-shaped flowers. For success with these beauties, provide a shaded location and rich, well-drained soil. Water regularly and feed in spring and fall.

Scale

Scale-infested plants will have brownish bumps on the stems. The tough outer coating on scale protects the small insect inside, which sucks plant juices from the stem. If left untreated, the scale will eventually produce a sticky, honeydew secretion which attracts ants and a blackish mold. If the infestation is not large, simply scrape the scale off the plant using the edge of a dull knife. Attract such natural predators as lacewing larvae and beneficial wasps (see page 150) to avoid problems with scale.

Slugs and Snails

If you wake up in the morning and find that something has eaten major portions of your bleeding heart's new growth—leaving slime trails—you'll know the culprits are slugs, snails or both. Although some natural controls work, even the most ardent organic gardeners have begun using a product called Escar-Go (which contains iron phosphate, a naturally occurring soil element—see page 145), to control snails and slugs. Chemical controls include products (usually in bait form) containing metaldehyde or methiocarb (see page 148). No matter what control you use, scatter it all around potential targets and any damp, shady spot where slugs and snails hide during the day. If you know there are slugs or snails in your area, always treat your garden with a control before their damage is apparent; slugs and snails can do a tremendous amount of damage in just one night.

Stem Rot

Stem rot causes bleeding heart stems to turn black at their bases, possibly with a covering of mold. Foliage will turn yellow; plants eventually fall over and die. Dig up and destroy any infected plants. Avoid the problem in the future by improving soil drainage with the incorporation of plenty of organic matter. If you use a mulch, keep it an inch or so away from the stems of the plants and allow the soil to dry out slightly between waterings.

Bleeding hearts combine beautifully with other shade-loving plants like hostas and ferns.

Digitalis
FOXGLOVE

Biennial or perennial, depending on species Zones 4–9

Foxglove Anthracnose

Foxglove anthracnose causes small, brownish, oddly-shaped spots on leaves. Foliage eventually turns yellow and dies. Prune off and destroy any infected foliage. Because this fungus harbors in garden debris from one year to the next, be sure to clean the garden thoroughly in the fall. Lessen the presence of foxglove anthracnose by allowing the soil to dry out somewhat between waterings, and by avoiding overhead watering.

Fusarium Wilt

Fusarium wilt is a frustrating soil-borne disease that causes foxglove plants to turn yellow, or individual leaves to turn brown. The plant eventually dies. Avoid the problem by incorporating plenty of leafmold or peat moss into the soil to improve soil drainage. If fusarium wilt attacks, completely remove and discard the affected plant, along with any soil the roots have come in contact with. If fusarium wilt has previously been a problem, plant foxglove in another location. If practical, solarize the soil (see page 151) to control soil-borne diseases.

Foxglove prefer a full-sun location, but will do fine in a partially shaded location as well. Plant in rich garden loam and keep evenly moist; fertilize once in spring.

Foxglove come in shades of rose, pink and white, and heights from 1 to 6 feet tall.

Thrips

Thrips damage appears as silvery or brown spots or streaking on leaves and flowers. To start, knock thrips off with a strong blast of water. If they persist, use an insecticidal soap or azadirachtin (see pages 142 and 144).

Verticillium Wilt

Verticillium wilt will cause foxglove foliage to turn yellow with brown blotches. Portions of the plant may wilt suddenly. A fungal disease, verticillium wilt lives in garden soil from one year to the next. If it's been a problem before, try planting foxglove in a different garden location. At the first sign of attack, make an application of liquid fertilizer; the resulting boost in growth may keep the plants from succumbing to the disease.

Echinacea
PURPLE CONEFLOWER

Zones 4–9

Perennial

Japanese Beetles

If you see small holes eaten right through the leaves of coneflowers, the culprit is likely to be Japanese beetles. These beetles are metallic green or brownish and about $1/2$ inch long. Control with insecticidal soap (see page 144). Control future generations with milky spores which kill the grubs as they overwinter in the soil (see page 151). Chemical controls include products that contain acephate, carbaryl or malathion (see pages 146 and 148).

Powdery Mildew

Powdery mildew may become a problem during periods of humid weather. Although the disease is not fatal, its signature powdery white coating on foliage and flowers is unattractive. Remove and destroy any infected plants. Prevent further outbreaks of powdery mildew with a spray of liquid sulfur (see page 145).

Texas Root Rot

Texas root rot will cause coneflowers to wilt suddenly and eventually die. Heavy, alkaline soils promote the presence of this fungal disease. Dig up and destroy any infected plants. Avoid the problem in the future by incorporating plenty of organic matter into the soil and adjusting its pH with garden sulfur (available at local garden centers); apply according to label directions.

Purple coneflowers are very sturdy plants, content with a full-sun location and average soil, water and feeding.

Butterflies love purple coneflowers because their open-faced flowers make excellent "landing pads."

Gladiolus
GLADIOLUS

Tender perennial, often grown as an annual

All Zones

Aphids

Aphids—masses of small tan, green or black insects—sometimes congregate on the new gladiolus growth. To start control, knock aphids off with a strong blast of water. If they persist, use an insecticidal soap or azadirachtin (see pages 142 and 144). Chemical controls include products that contain acephate or malathion (see pages 146-148).

Borers

Borers, as their name suggests, bore holes in the main stems of plants and live inside, eating the plants from the inside out. If sections of plants suddenly wilt, despite sufficient water, check for small holes in the stems surrounded by a fine sawdust-like material called frass. About all you can do: Dig up and destroy any infected plants or portions of plants.

Botrytis Blight

Botrytis blight causes spots all over gladiolus foliage and flowers. Once infected, gladiolus corms may rot. Cool temperatures and high humidity exacerbate the problem. About the only preventative measures are to dig up and destroy infected corms and to apply a layer of organic mulch over the garden bed.

Bulb Mites

Bulb mites are very small insects that burrow into gladiolus corms, transmitting diseases that either keep the bulbs from sprouting or cause them to have yellow foliage. Gladiolus corms infected with mites may rot in storage. Dispose of any soft or rotting corms immediately. You can help control bulb mites by attracting their natural predators with such plants as alyssum and scabiosa.

Dry Rot

Dry rot causes reddish brown spots of rot to appear on bulbs; if the bulb sprouts, the plant will probably have yellowed foliage and few flowers. Dry rot is most prevalent in poorly drained, cold soils. Dispose of any infected bulbs. Avoid the problem by planting bulbs in light, well-drained soil. Let dug bulbs dry in a warm, breezy place for a couple of days before storing.

Gladiolus Thrips

The damage from these tiny insects shows up as silvery streaking on leaves and as distorted new growth; flowers infected with thrips may fail to open. This is usually a problem during periods of hot, dry weather. Begin control by knocking thrips off foliage with a strong blast of water. If the problem persists, spray with an insecticide containing carbaryl, acephate or dimethoate (see pages 146-149). Avoid the problem by dusting the bulbs with carbaryl before storing for the winter.

The tall, dramatic spikes of gladiolus—in an amazing array of colors—have been a favorite of flower arrangers for generations. For best flowers, plant in a full-sun location in a rich garden loam. Provide regular watering and one feeding, after the plants have bloomed.

Tarnished Plant Bugs

Tarnished plant bugs are most active in the early spring but may persist through summer. As they feed on foliage, they inject toxins into the plant, which results in deformed foliage and flowers, both of which may eventually turn black. Control tarnished plant bugs with a spray of insecticidal soap (see page 144).

Gypsophila
BABY'S BREATH

Perennial Zones 3–9

Crown Gall

A swelling around the base of the main stem of baby's breath is a strange affliction called crown gall, caused by harmful bacteria. Plants infected with crown gall do not grow well; most will eventually die. There's not much you can do to deter the infection except dig up and destroy infected plants. To avoid the problem in the future, remove all soil touched by the roots of infected plants, and solarize planting beds (see page 151) before replanting with susceptible plants.

Slugs and Snails

If you find that something has eaten major portions of your baby's breath new growth—and has left slime trails in the process—you'll know the culprits are slugs, snails or both. Although there are a number of more-or-less effective natural controls, even the most ardent organic gardeners have begun using a product called Escar-Go (which contains iron phosphate, a naturally occurring soil element—see page 145), to control these frustrating pests. Chemical controls include products (usually in bait form) containing metaldehyde or methiocarb (see page 148).

Whether using Escar-Go or a chemical control, scatter it all around potential targets and any damp, shady spot where slugs and snails hide during the day. If you know there are slugs or snails in your area, always treat your garden with a control before their damage is apparent; slugs and snails can do a tremendous amount of damage in even one night.

Baby's breath is another favorite of flower arrangers and very easy to grow. Plant in a full-sun location, in average soil. Somewhat drought tolerant once established, baby's breath only needs one annual feeding in spring.

Aster Leafhoppers

If you notice small, distorted, yellowish leaves on your baby's breath, the problem is a virus known as aster yellows. Aster yellows is spread by aster leafhoppers (also known as the six-spotted leafhopper). To control the virus, you have to control the leafhoppers. Start by picking off any affected growth and disposing of it. Remove the leafhoppers with a strong blast of water, or use an insecticidal soap (see page 144); in either case, be sure to hit both the tops and bottoms of the leaves for complete control. Chemical controls for leafhoppers include products containing acephate, carbaryl or malathion (see pages 146-148).

Aster Yellows

Aster yellows (see above) occasionally attacks baby's breath. Affected leaves will be weakened and have a mottled yellow appearance. Since there is no cure for this disease, simply remove and destroy any affected plants. Wash hands with soap and hot water after touching foliage affected with aster yellows, because simply touching leaves and flowers of healthy plants can spread the disease. If you use pruning shears to cut out affected foliage, dip the blades in rubbing alcohol after use to disinfect.

Baby's breath is not only a good filler in cut flower bouquets, it also performs the same function in the flower border.

Helianthus
SUNFLOWER

Annuals and perennials

Annuals: All Zones

Perennials: Zones 6–9

Aphids

Aphids—masses of small tan, green or black insects—sometimes congregate on the new growth of sunflowers. To start, knock aphids off with a strong blast of water. If they persist, use an insecticidal soap or azadirachtin (see pages 142 and 144). Chemical controls include products that contain acephate, diazinon or malathion (see pages 146-148).

Powdery Mildew

Sunflowers will occasionally be bothered by powdery mildew if growing conditions turn humid. Although the disease is not fatal, its signature powdery white coating on foliage and flowers is unattractive. Remove and destroy any infected plants. Prevent further outbreaks of powdery mildew with a spray of liquid sulfur (see page 145).

With a sunny face like this, it's easy to see how sunflowers got their name.

Rust

If sunflower leaves turn yellow and show powdery orange-brown spots, the plants have become infected with the disease known as rust. Rust is spread by the wind, and the best control is to remove any infected foliage (or whole plants) as soon as the disease makes an appearance. To prevent further problems, spray plants with a sulfur mixture (see page 145).

Sunflower Beetles

Sunflower beetles attack tender young sunflower seedlings, feeding on their leaves. Their damage can be confused with problems caused by slugs and snails. Look closely: If the damage is caused by sunflower beetles you'll notice yellow-striped beetles in the area. The actual feeding is done by the larvae of the beetles—small yellow-green nymphs that feed at night. Control nymphs with a spray of insecticidal soap (see page 144).

Tarnished Plant Bugs

Tarnished plant bugs are most active in the early spring but may persist through summer. As they feed on foliage, they inject toxins into the plant, which results in deformed foliage and flowers, which may eventually turn black. Control tarnished plant bugs with a spray of insecticidal soap (see page 144).

Woollybear Caterpillars

The tender new leaves of sunflowers are favorite fodder for the yellow woollybear caterpillars. If you notice these caterpillars feeding on your plants, remove them by hand or spray with Btk (*B.t.* var. *kurstaki*), see page 143.

Sunflowers are among the most willing of all garden plants, requiring only a full-sun location and average soil, water and feeding.

Sunflowers have enjoyed an increase in popularity recently, resulting in a wider array of varieties, forms and colors—including deep orange and mahogany.

Hemerocallis
DAYLILIES

Perennial   Zones 3–9

Daylilies may be the easiest of all perennial flowers to grow: They'll accept full sun to fairly heavy shade, all types of soil, and infrequent watering and feeding. Even with neglect, they put on a wonderful show of color every year—year after year. Shown here: 'Betty Loves Me'.

Aphids

Aphids, those masses of small tan, green or black insects, sometimes congregate on the new growth of daylilies. Start control by knocking aphids off with a strong blast of water. If they persist, use an insecticidal soap or azadirachtin (see pages 142 and 144). Chemical controls include products which contain acephate or malathion (see pages 146-148).

Bacterial Soft Rot

Luckily, this problem is fairly rare. In heavy, poorly drained soil—especially during extended periods of wet weather—the foliage and flowers of daylilies may start to rot. Because this condition can spread quickly, dig up and destroy any infected plants at the first sign of attack. Then clean your shovels and pruning shears with rubbing alcohol to prevent spreading the disease to healthy plants. To avoid the problem in the future, incorporate plenty of organic soil amendments to the beds to improve drainage.

Harmful Nematodes

Harmful nematodes—microscopic, soil-borne worms—cause stunted or distorted growth. Foliage wilts, turns yellow and whole plants eventually die. If you pull up a plant, you'll notice stunted roots with small knots or lumps on them. Dig up and destroy any affected plants. Solarize the soil (see page 151) to avoid the problem in the future, and incorporate plenty of organic soil amendments into the planting bed. Nematrol has shown some success in controlling nematodes, as does incorporating chitin into the soil (see page 143).

Spider Mites

Spider mites can attack daylilies, especially during periods of hot, dry weather. Telltale damage includes stippled, grayish foliage and stunted growth. The mites attack the undersides of leaves and usually leave small holes and fine webbing in their wake. Blast mites off with a strong spray of water, paying particular attention to the undersides of the leaves. If the problem persists, use an insecticidal soap (see page 144) specially formulated for the control of mites.

Thrips

Thrips damage appears as silvery or brown spots or streaking on leaves and flowers. First, knock thrips off with a strong blast of water. If thrips persist, use an insecticidal soap or azadirachtin (see pages 142 and 144).

Daylilies are easy to grow and easy to hybridize as well. This trait results in many new daylily varieties every year. Shown here 'Bright Sunset'.

Heuchera
CORALBELLS

Perennial   Zones 3–9

Leaf Spot

Leaf spot appears on coralbell foliage as grayish white spots with darker rings. Prevalent during periods of warm, humid weather, this disease can be lessened by immediately removing and disposing of any infected leaves, avoiding overhead watering, and permitting good air circulation between plants. Also, space plants generously .

Mealybugs

You'll definitely know if your coralbells have mealybugs: their distinctive fuzzy white bodies (about $1/4$ inch long) look like nothing else in the pest world. If you notice mealybugs on the foliage, start control by knocking them off with a strong blast of water. If the infestation continues, spray with an insecticidal soap, paying special attention to the undersides of leaves (see page 144). Chemical controls include products containing malathion or carbaryl (see pages 146-148).

Coralbells are extremely long-lived perennials, with few demands other than a full-sun to partially shaded location, average garden soil, and once-a-year feeding in spring. Does best with regular waterings.

Powdery Mildew

Although the disease is not fatal, its powdery white coating on foliage and flowers is unattractive. Remove and destroy any infected plants. Prevent further outbreaks of powdery mildew with a spray of liquid sulfur (see page 145).

Rust

If coralbell leaves turn yellow and show powdery orange-brown spots, the plants are suffering from the disease known as rust. Spread by the wind, rust is best controled by removing any infected foliage (or whole plants) as soon as the disease makes an appearance. To prevent further problems, spray plants with a sulfur mixture (see page 145).

Stem Rot

Stem rot causes coralbell stems to turn black at their bases, possibly with a covering of mold. Foliage will turn yellow; plants eventually fall over and die. Begin control by digging up and destroying any infected plants. Avoid the problem in the future by improving soil drainage: incorporate plenty of organic matter. If you use a mulch, keep it an inch or so away from the stems of the plants and allow the soil to dry out slightly between waterings.

Strawberry Root Weevils

These $1/4$-inch-long weevils have a particular interest in coralbells, chewing on foliage and eating the crowns of the plants, turning them black. Affected plants will eventually die. Dig up and destroy any infected plants. Avoid further problems with strawberry root weevils by applying beneficial nematodes (see page 150) to the bed in spring, with an additional application in summer.

Coralbells have been a favorite border plant for years. Recently they've been discovered as a very attractive and long-lasting cut flower.

Hosta
FUNKIA, PLANTAIN LILY

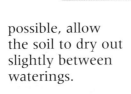

Zones 3–9

Perennial

Crown Rot

Although hostas thrive in the shade, they don't like heavy, poorly drained soil. These conditions foster bacteria which cause crown or root rot, turning hosta foliage yellow and encouraging the possible presence of web-like strands of fungus at the base of the plants. Dig up and destroy infected plants at the first sign of attack. To avoid future problems, incorporate plenty of organic matter into the soil to improve drainage. If possible, allow the soil to dry out slightly between waterings.

Scale

Scale-infested plants will have brownish bumps on the leaves. The tough outer coating on scale protects the small insect inside, which does damage by sucking plant juices from the stems. If left untreated, the scale will eventually produce a sticky, honeydew secretion which attracts ants and a blackish fungus. If the infestation is not large, simply scrape the scale off the plant using the edge of a dull knife or a plastic scouring pad. To avoid problems with scale, attract such natural predators as lacewing larvae and beneficial wasps (see page 150).

Slugs and Snails

If something has eaten major portions of your hosta's new growth—and has left telltale slime trails—you'll know the culprits are slugs, snails or both. Although there are a number of natural controls, even the most ardent organic gardeners have begun using Escar-Go, which contains iron phosphate, a naturally occurring soil element (see page 145), to control these frustrating pests. Chemical controls include products (usually in bait form) containing metaldehyde or methiocarb (see page 148). Whether using Escar-Go or a chemical control, scatter it all around potential targets and any damp, shady spot where slugs and snails hide during the day. If you know there are slugs or snails in your area, always treat your garden with a control before their damage is apparent; slugs and snails can do a tremendous amount of damage in even one night.

Every year brings more hosta varieties, expanding an already bewildering selection—from short to tall—in subtle shades of green, from blue-green to chartreuse, and every variation in between. Shown here: 'Frances Williams'.

Hostas are very hardy and easy-to-grow perennials. They accept all manner of shaded conditions, from dappled sunlight to heavy shade. For best results, plant in a soil amended with plenty of organic soil amendments, kept evenly moist. Feed yearly, in spring.

Few plants flower in the shade as spectacularly as hostas.

Hyacinthus
HYACINTH

Perennial, grown from a bulb

Zones 4–9

Aphids

Aphids—masses of small tan, green or black insects—sometimes congregate on the new growth of hyacinth. Start control by knocking aphids off with a strong blast of water. If they persist, use an insecticidal soap or azadirachtin (see pages 142 and 144). Chemical controls include products that contain acephate or malathion (see pages 146-148).

Bulb Mites

Bulb mites are very small insects that burrow into hyacinth bulbs, transmitting diseases that either keep the bulbs from sprouting or cause them to have yellow foliage. Hyacinth bulbs infected with mites may rot in storage. Dispose of any soft or rotting corms immediately. To help control bulb mites, attract their natural predators with such plants as alyssum and scabiosa.

Bacterial Soft Rot

If your hyacinth bulbs fail to bloom, and the foliage develops rotten spots, you've got a case of bacterial soft rot. Here's how to avoid the problem: Allow the soil to dry out slightly between waterings, by incorporating plenty of organic matter into the soil to improve drainage, and by spacing bulbs generously to increase air circulation. Once the disease strikes, the only solution is to dig up and destroy any infected plants.

Botrytis Blight

Botrytis blight (also called gray mold) causes small black spots on hyacinth leaves and flowers, and possibly the presence of a grayish mold. Periods of cool, wet weather encourage this fungus. You can avoid the problem by allowing the soil to dry out slightly between waterings, incorporating plenty of organic matter into the soil to improve drainage, and by spacing bulbs generously to increase air circulation. Once the disease strikes, the only solution is to dig up and destroy any infected plants.

Hyacinths do best in full sun and a well-drained garden loam. The tall, densely-packed flower heads are intensely fragrant and are available in shades of purple, rose, pink, pale yellow and white.

Ornithogalum Mosaic Virus

Sucking insects spread this viral disease. Infected plants will have light-colored streaks in the leaves and they may wilt suddenly. Control sucking insects with a spray of insecticidal soap (see page 144). Dig up and destroy any infected bulbs.

Stem and Bulb Nematodes

Stem and bulb nematodes—microscopic, soil-borne worms—cause stunted growth and yellow foliage. Affected plants eventually die. If you pull up a plant, you'll notice stunted roots with small knots or lumps on them. Dig up and destroy any affected plants. Avoid the problem in the future by solarizing the soil (see page 151) and by incorporating plenty of organic soil amendments into the planting bed. The product Nematrol has shown some success in controlling southern root-knot nematodes, as does incorporating chitin into the soil (see page 143).

Iberis
CANDYTUFT

Perennial   Zones 3–9

Candytuft is a great, low-growing perennial, perfect for edging flower beds, walkways or rock gardens. Plant in full sun to light shade in average garden soil with regular watering and a yearly feeding in spring.

Diamondback Moths

Chewed leaves and serpentine tan trails on the foliage of candytuft are the signs of an infestation of diamondback moth larvae. These small, yellow-green caterpillars favor new growth for mining, eventually eating the older foliage. Control the larvae with a spray of Bt (see page 143).

Powdery Mildew

Candytuft will occasionally be bothered by powdery mildew if growing conditions turn humid. Although the disease is not fatal, its signature powdery white coating on foliage and flowers is unattractive. Remove and destroy any infected plants. Prevent further outbreaks of powdery mildew with a spray of liquid sulfur (see page 145).

Very long-flowering, candytuft is available in a wide array of colors from lavender, pink and purple to rose, crimson and white.

Impatiens
IMPATIENS

Annual   All Zones

Aphids

Aphids, those masses of small tan, green or black insects, sometimes congregate on the new growth of impatiens. Start control by knocking aphids off with a strong blast of water. If they persist, use an insecticidal soap or azadirachtin (see pages 142 and 144). Chemical controls include products that contain acephate or malathion.

Bacterial Wilt

If your impatiens suddenly wilt, even though there's sufficient moisture in the soil, bacterial wilt is the probable cause—especially if there's been an extended period of warm weather. Dig up and destroy any infected plants at the first sign of attack. Remove all soil touched by the roots. Avoid problems in the future by incorporating plenty of organic matter to the planting beds and by keeping them free of garden debris. Do not overcrowd plants, to maximize air circulation.

Spider Mites

Spider mites can attack impatiens, especially during periods of

Relatively new on the scene are the New Guinea hybrid impatiens. They have intensely colored flowers and most have brilliantly colored, variegated foliage. They differ from the more common impatiens (I. wallerana) in that they prefer full sun.

hot, dry weather. Telltale damage includes stippled, grayish foliage and stunted growth. The mites attack the undersides of leaves and usually leave small holes and fine webbing in their wake. Blast mites off with a strong spray of water, paying particular attention to the undersides of the leaves. If the problem persists, use an insecticidal soap (see page 144) specially formulated for the control of mites.

Spotted Cucumber Beetles

Spotted cucumber beetles munch on impatiens leaves and flowers, leaving holes or ragged edges. The beetles themselves are about $1/4$ inch long, yellowish green in color, with black spots. Beneficial nematodes will help prevent spotted cucumber beetles (see page 150). Chemical controls include products that contain carbaryl or pyrethrins (see pages 146-149).

Southern Root-Knot Nematodes

Stem and bulb nematodes—microscopic, soil-borne worms—cause stunted growth and

yellow foliage. Affected plants eventually die. If you pull up a plant, you'll see stunted roots with small knots or lumps. Dig up and destroy any affected plants. To avoid the problem in the future, solarize the soil (see page 151) and incorporate plenty of organic soil amendments into the planting bed. The product Nematrol has shown some success in controlling southern root-knot nematodes, as does incorporating chitin into the soil (see page 143).

Tarnished Plant Bugs

Tarnished plant bugs are most active in the early spring but may persist through summer. As they feed on foliage, these bugs inject toxins that deform foliage and may cause the leaves to eventually turn black. Control tarnished plant bugs with a spray of insecticidal soap (see page 144).

Impatiens are probably the best flowering annual for shaded garden locations. Plant in a garden loam with plenty of organic soil amendment, keep evenly moist and fertilize monthly throughout the growing season. Impatiens do well in all types of shade. Shown here: 'Blitz'.

Iris
IRIS

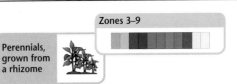

Zones 3–9

Perennials, grown from a rhizome

For all their beauty and willingness to bloom, iris make few demands on the gardener. Plant in a full-sun location, in a well-drained soil. Iris are not particular about water; fertilize them yearly, each spring.

Bacterial Soft Rot

In heavy, poorly drained soil—especially during extended periods of wet weather—iris foliage and flowers may start to rot. Because this condition can spread quickly, dig up and destroy any infected plants at the first sign of attack. Clean shovels and pruning shears used in removal with rubbing alcohol to prevent spreading the disease to healthy plants. To avoid the problem in the future, incorporate plenty of organic soil amendment to the beds to improve drainage.

Iris Borers

If you notice small holes or chewed spots in the leaves of your iris—along with the presence of a fine, dust-like substance called frass— the problem is iris borers. Dig up and destroy any infected plants. Avoid the problem in the future by applying beneficial nematodes (see page 150) to the soil. If borers are a persistent problem, plant resistant varieties (see page 21).

Slugs and Snails

When you discover something has eaten major portions of your iris's new growth—and left slime trails—you'll know the culprits are slugs, snails or both. Although there are some effective natural controls to try, even the most ardent organic gardeners use a product called Escar-Go, which contains iron phosphate, a naturally occurring soil element (see page 145), to control these frustrating pests. Chemical controls include products (usually in bait form) containing metaldehyde or methiocarb (see page 148). Whether using Escar-Go or a chemical control, scatter it all around potential targets and any damp, shady spot where slugs and snails hide during the day. If you know there are slugs or snails in your area, always treat your garden with a control before their damage is apparent; slugs and snails can do a tremendous amount of damage in even one night.

Thrips

Thrips damage appears as silvery or brown spots or streaking on leaves and flowers. Start by knocking thrips off with a strong blast of water. If thrips persist, use an insecticidal soap or azadirachtin (see pages 142 and 144).

The array of colors and color combinations available in bearded iris is incredible. Every year new named varieties make their debut, tempting gardeners with even more choices.

Breeding efforts have produce bearded iris in a variety of sizes, from dwarf to full-sized. Shown here is a miniature dwarf iris, growing no more than 10 inches tall.

Lathyrus
SWEET PEA

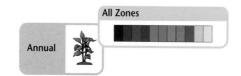

Annual | All Zones

If you want as many sweet pea flowers as possible, plant them in a rich garden loam, keep it evenly moist, and feed monthly with a complete fertilizer. Sweet peas do best in a full-sun location.

Damping Off

Because almost all sweet peas are planted from seed, damping off is a common problem. This frustrating disease causes young seedlings to simply fall over and die. It's caused by soil-borne fungi, particularly in heavy, poorly drained planting beds. Avoid the problem by incorporating plenty of organic matter into the soil to improve drainage; allow the bed to dry out slightly between waterings.

Leafrollers and Leaftiers

If you notice that individual sweet pea leaves are folded or rolled, with or without fine webbing, the problem is leafrollers or leaftiers. Unroll one of the leaves and you'll probably catch the culprits in action: small green, brown or yellow caterpillars. Pick off and discard any affected leaves. Control with sprays is difficult because the caterpillars are protected by the rolled or folded leaves. Chemical controls include products containing acephate or carbaryl (see page 146).

Powdery Mildew

Although the disease is not fatal, its signature powdery white coating on foliage and flowers is unattractive. Remove and destroy any infected plants. Prevent further outbreaks of powdery mildew with a spray of liquid sulfur (see page 145).

Bacterial Fasciation

This strange disease is caused by soil-borne bacteria and produces wide, flattened stems—as if several plants have been fused together. Dig up and destroy any infected plants. To avoid the problem in the future: solarize the planting bed (see page 151).

Botrytis Blight

Botrytis blight (also called gray mold) causes a grayish mold to form on sweet pea leaves and flowers. This fungus is encouraged by periods of cool, humid weather. To keep the problem from occurring, avoid overhead watering, incorporate plenty of organic matter into the soil to improve drainage, and space plants generously to increase air circulation. Once the disease strikes, the only solution is to dig up and destroy any infected plants.

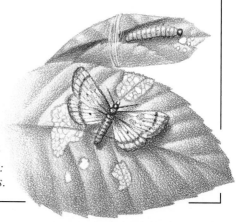

Leaftiers will occasionally attack sweet peas. If you notice rolled or folded leaves with small caterpillars hiding inside, the culprits are leaftiers or leafrollers. Easiest control: Simply pick off and destroy any affected leaves.

Lilium
LILY

To produce their magnificent flowers, lilies need a little extra care: The best planting locations are where the lily will have its roots in the shade and its head in the sun. Plant in a garden loam, with plenty of organic soil amendment worked in. Keep soil evenly moist but not wet. Shown here: 'Coralbee'.

Aphids

Aphids, those masses of small tan, green or black insects, sometimes congregate on the new growth of lilies. Start control by knocking aphids off with a strong blast of water. If they persist, use an insecticidal soap or azadirachtin (see pages 142 and 144). Chemical controls include products that contain acephate or malathion (see pages 146-148).

Borers

Borers, as their name suggests, bore holes in the main stems of plants and live inside, eating the plants from the inside out. If sections of plants suddenly wilt, despite sufficient water, check for telltale small holes in the stems surrounded by a fine sawdust-like material called frass. About all that can be done is to dig up and destroy any infected plants or portions of plants.

Lily Botrytis Blight

Lily botrytis blight causes lily leaves to wilt, turn black and possibly become covered with a grayish mold. This fungus is encouraged by periods of cool, humid weather. To keep the problem from occurring, avoid overhead watering, incorporate plenty of organic matter into the soil to improve drainage, and space plants generously to increase air circulation. Once the disease strikes, you'll have to dig up and destroy any infected plants.

Narcissus Bulb Flies

Narcissus bulb flies look like small black, brown and yellow bumblebees. These flies' larvae eat lily bulbs, causing holes and rot, along with a lack of growth and a scarcity of flowers. Do not plant any soft bulbs, or bulbs that show any signs of rot. Before planting, dust healthy bulbs with an insecticide containing trichlorfon. Make another application of the insecticide after the bulbs have been planted, but before covering them with soil. In early summer, drench the soil and the lily leaves with a solution of water and the insecticide, following label directions.

Red Lily Leaf Beetles

Holes in the leaves of your lily plants, along with the presence of small black larvae or bright red beetles, indicate red lily leaf beetles. Keep your eye out for their damage, because they can cause serious trouble and do so in a hurry. Control at the first sign of attack with an insecticide containing azadirachtin (see page 142).

Root Rot

If the base of a lily plant starts rotting and turning black, the problem is root rot. Dig up and discard infected plants at the first sign of attack. Prevention: Plant lilies in a very well drained soil, amended with plenty of compost, leafmold or peat moss.

Viruses

If your lily plants or flowers are stunted with mottled, streaked or unusually colored foliage, the problem is a virus. Since there is no cure for viral diseases, dig up and destroy any infected plants at the first sign of attack. Help avoid viral diseases by controlling insects, such as aphids and leafhoppers, that spread viruses as they suck on plants. A spray of insecticidal soap will control both aphids and leafhoppers (see page 144).

Lobelia
LOBELIA

Annual   All Zones

Aphids

Small tan, green or black insects—aphids—sometimes congregate on the new growth of lobelia. Knock aphids off with a strong blast of water. If they persist, use an insecticidal soap or azadirachtin (see pages 142 and 144). Chemical controls include products that contain acephate or malathion (see pages 146-148).

Aster Leafhoppers

If you notice distorted, yellowish leaves with brown edges on your lobelia plants, the problem is a virus known as aster yellows. The problem is spread by aster leafhoppers (also known as the six-spotted leafhopper), so to control the disease you have to control the leafhoppers. Start by picking off any affected growth and disposing of it. Remove the leafhoppers with a strong blast of water, using an insecticidal soap or light horticultural oil, which will smother the insects. Chemical controls for leafhoppers include products containing acephate, carbaryl or malathion (see pages 146-148). With any control, be sure to hit both the tops and bottoms of the leaves for complete control.

Leaf Spot

Leaf spot, appearing on lobelia foliage as various-sized spots in a variety of colors, is prevalent during periods of warm, humid weather; you must immediately remove and dispose of any infected leaves, avoid overhead watering, and permit good air circulation between plants with generous spacing.

Redbanded Leafrollers

Damaged leaves, some of which may be rolled or held together with fine webbing, indicate the presence of leafrollers— the brown, green or yellow caterpillars of the redbanded moth. About the only control is to cut off and discard any damaged leaves at the first sign of attack.

Root Rot

If the base of a lobelia plant starts rotting right at the soil line, the problem is root rot. Dig up and discard infected plants at the first sign of attack. Avoid the problem by planting lobelias in a very well drained soil, amended with plenty of compost, leafmold or peat moss.

Wireworms

Wireworms cause lobelia foliage to yellow and die; occasionally, whole plants will be eaten off at the base. The culprits—the white, yellow or brown larvae of the clicking beetle—live in the soil and eat roots. Spread a layer of wood ashes over the affected area to control, or make an application of beneficial nematodes (see page 150).

One of the best of all the trailing, flowering annuals, lobelia does best in a lightly shaded location. Plant in a rich garden loam, kept evenly moist and fertilized monthly.

Lobularia maritima
SWEET ALYSSUM

Annual
All Zones

Sweet alyssum may be the classic annual for edging flower beds and walkways. It prefers a full-sun location but will accept light shade. Not particular about its soil, sweet alyssum is fairly drought tolerant once established.

Cutworms

If the new growth of your sweet alyssum plants is cut off right at soil level, you've probably got cutworms. Nocturnal feeders, these 1- to 2-inch-long worms can cause a lot of damage in just one night. If you've had problems with cutworms in the past, it's best to avoid their damage with preventative measures; one easy way is to make protective collars (see page 151), or apply Bt granules (see page 143) to the soil just as the new growth starts to appear. Chemical controls include products with the active ingredient acephate (see page 146).

Root Rot

If you notice the base of your alyssum plants rotting and turning black, the problem is root rot. Dig up and discard infected plants. To avoid the problem, plant alyssum in a very well drained soil that is amended with plenty of compost, leafmold or peat moss.

Southern Root-Knot Nematodes

Southern root-knot nematodes—microscopic, soil-borne worms—cause stunted growth and yellow foliage. Affected plants eventually die. If you pull up a plant, you'll notice stunted roots with small knots or lumps on them. Dig up and destroy any affected plants. Avoid the problem in the future by solarizing the soil (see page 151) and by incorporating plenty of organic soil amendments into the planting bed. The product Nematrol has shown some success in controlling southern root-knot nematodes, as does incorporating chitin into the soil (see page 143).

Aster Yellows

Aster yellows, a viral disease, occasionally attacks sweet alyssum. Affected leaves will be weakened and have a mottled yellow appearance. Since there is no cure for this disease, simply remove and destroy any affected plants. Wash hands with soap and hot water after touching foliage affected with aster yellows, because the affliction can be spread by simply touching leaves and flowers of healthy plants. If you use pruning shears to cut out affected foliage, dip the blades in rubbing alcohol after use to disinfect.

Lupinus
LUPINE

Annual or perennial, depending on species

All Zones

It's hard to imagine more brilliantly colored flowers than these Russell hybrid lupines. Plant lupines in a full-sun location, in a rich, well-drained garden loam. Keep soil evenly moist; fertilize once, a week or so after planting.

Prevent further outbreaks of powdery mildew with a spray of liquid sulfur (see page 145).

Rust

If lupine leaves turn yellow and show powdery orange-brown spots, the plants have become infected with rust. Spread by the wind, rust is best controlled by removing any infected foliage (or whole plants) as soon as the disease makes an appearance. To prevent further problems, spray plants with a sulfur solution (see page 145).

Whiteflies

If your lupine plants are lacking in vigor, are pale, and if clouds of very small white insects fly up when the leaves are disturbed, you've got whiteflies. To control them, either use an insecticidal soap (see page 144), or simply blast the whiteflies off the plants with a strong spray of water.

Aphids

Tiny tan, green or black aphids sometimes congregate on the new growth of lupines. Knock aphids off with a strong blast of water. If they persist, use an insecticidal soap or azadirachtin (see pages 142 and 144). Chemical controls include products that contain acephate or malathion.

Leaf Spot

Leaf spot appears on lupine foliage as grayish white spots with darker rings. Prevalent during periods of warm, humid weather, this disease can be lessened by immediately removing and disposing of any in-fected leaves, avoiding overhead watering and permitting good air circulation between plants with generous spacing.

Powdery Mildew

Lupines will occasionally be bothered by powdery mildew if growing conditions turn humid. Although the disease is not fatal, its powdery white coating is unattractive. Remove and destroy any infected plants.

The alternating white and purple rows give these lupines an interesting texture, quite unlike any other flower.

Myosotis
FORGET-ME-NOT

Annual or biennial · **All Zones**

Botrytis Blight

Botrytis blight (also called gray mold) causes stems and flowers of forget-me-nots to rot and possibly become covered with a grayish mold. Periods of cool, humid weather encourage this fungus. You can keep the problem from occurring by avoiding overhead watering, incorporating plenty of organic matter into the soil to improve drainage, and by spacing plants generously to increase air circulation. Once the disease strikes, you'll have to dig up and destroy any infected plants.

Crown Rot

Forget-me-nots don't like heavy, poorly drained soil. These conditions foster bacteria which encourage crown or root rot, causing foliage to wilt and turn brown. Dig up and destroy infected plants at the first sign of attack. Incorporate plenty of organic matter into the soil to improve drainage to avoid future problems. If possible, allow the soil to dry out slightly between waterings.

Green Peach Aphids

Green peach aphids—clustered colonies of small tan, green or gray insects—sometimes congregate on the new growth of forget-me-nots. Start control by knocking aphids off with a strong blast of water. If they persist, use an insecticidal soap or azadirachtin (see pages 142 and 144). Chemical controls include products that contain acephate or malathion.

Potato Flea Beetles

Potato flea beetles are very small, shiny black beetles that produce small holes ($1/8$-inch) in the leaves of forget-me-nots. The beetles jump around like fleas when disturbed. Affected foliage may wilt and eventually die. Control with a spray of insecticidal soap (see page 144). Other controls include insecticides containing pyrethrin, carbaryl or methoxychlor (see pages 146-149).

Forget-me-nots do best in a partially shaded garden location; they are not fussy about soil type, but keep the soil evenly moist. Where happy, forget-me-nots reseed readily.

Narcissus
DAFFODIL

Perennial, planted from a bulb

Zones 3–9

Few things announce spring more beautifully than daffodils. They prefer a full-sun location, well-drained soil kept evenly moist up to the time the bulb blooms, and feeding only at planting time. After flowering, do not tie up or braid foliage; allow it to grow for as long as possible.

Basal Rot

Basal rot is a soil-borne fungus that causes stunted foliage and rot in stored narcissus bulbs. Dig up and discard infected plants at the first sign of attack, including all of the soil that has come in contact with the roots. Plant narcissus in a very well drained soil, amended with plenty of compost, leafmold or peat moss. To avoid problems, solarize the planting bed (see page 151). Before storing bulbs, prepare a fungicide bath: Add 2 tablespoons of a fungicide containing benomyl to a gallon of warm water (water temperature should be 80°F), stir well, and allow narcissus bulbs to soak for 20 minutes. Allow bulbs to dry in a warm, dry place and store in a well-ventilated location with a more-or-less constant temperature of 60°F.

Narcissus Bulb Flies

Narcissus bulb flies look like small black, brown and yellow bumblebees. Larvae of these flies eat narcissus bulbs, causing holes and rot, along with a lack of growth and a scarcity of flowers. Do not plant any soft bulbs, or any bulbs showing signs of rot. Dust healthy bulbs with an insecticide containing trichlorfon before planting. Make another application of the insecticide after the bulb has been planted, but before covering it with soil. In early summer, drench the soil and the narcissus leaves with a solution of water and the insecticide, following label directions.

Narcissus Mosaic Virus

Narcissus mosaic virus causes pale streaks in narcissus foliage and flowers; plants become weak and may collapse. Viral diseases are difficult to control; it's easier to control the sucking insects which spread the disease with a spray of insecticidal soap (see page 144). Dig up and destroy any infected plants at the first sign of attack.

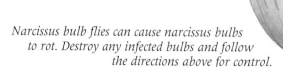

Narcissus bulb flies can cause narcissus bulbs to rot. Destroy any infected bulbs and follow the directions above for control.

The classic 'King Alfred' daffodil against a clear blue spring sky.

Stem Nematodes

Stem nematodes are microscopic, soil-borne worms which cause stunted growth and yellow foliage. Affected plants eventually die. If you pull up a plant, you'll notice stunted roots with small knots or lumps on them. Dig up and destroy any affected plants. Avoid the problem in the future by solarizing the soil (see page 151) and by incorporating plenty of organic soil amendments into the planting bed. The product Nematrol has shown some success in controlling southern root-knot nematodes.

Nicotiana
FLOWERING TOBACCO

Annual All Zones

Cutworms

If you find your young flowering tobacco plants cut off right at soil level, you've probably got cutworms. Nocturnal feeders, these 1- to 2-inch-long worms can cause a lot of damage in just one night. If you've had problems with cutworms in the past, it's best to avoid their damage with preventative measures; one easy way is to make protective collars (see page 151) or apply Bt granules (see page 143) to the soil just as the new growth starts to appear. Chemical controls include products with the active ingredient acephate (see page 146).

Colorado Potato Beetles

Colorado potato beetles and their larvae are voracious eaters and can defoliate nicotiana plants in a hurry. Avoid the problem by ridding the garden beds of all garden debris each fall. A spray of Btsd (*Bacillus thuringiensis* var. *san diego*) will kill the beetle nymphs and grubs (see page 143). Other controls include insecticides containing pyrethrin, rotenone, azadirachtin or carbaryl (see pages 146-149).

Downy Mildew

Flowering tobacco will occasionally be bothered by downy mildew, especially if growing conditions turn cool and damp. Although the disease is not fatal, its signature white, tan or black patches on leaves are unattractive. Remove and destroy any infected foliage. Space plants generously to increase air circulation. Prevent further outbreaks of downy mildew with a spray of liquid sulfur (see page 145).

Leaf Spot

Leaf spot appears on flowering tobacco foliage as grayish white spots with darker rings. Prevalent during periods of warm, humid weather, this

Nicotiana, or flowering tobacco, is an easy-to-grow annual with a very long season of bloom. Plant in full sun to part shade in a good garden loam. Water when necessary during the growing season; fertilize a week or so after planting.

Nicotiana flowers have a sweet fragrance, more pronounced during the evening than during the day. Shown here: 'Nicki'.

disease can be lessened by immediately removing and disposing of any infected leaves, avoiding overhead watering, and permitting good air circulation between plants with generous spacing.

Potato Flea Beetles

Potato flea beetles are very small, shiny black beetles that produce small holes ($1/8$-inch) in flowering tobacco leaves. The beetles jump around like fleas when disturbed. Affected foliage may wilt and eventually die. Control with a spray of insecticidal soap (see page 144). Other controls include insecticides containing pyrethrin, carbaryl or methoxychlor (see pages 146-149).

Powdery Mildew

Flowering tobacco will occasionally be bothered by powdery mildew if growing conditions turn cool and humid. Although the disease is not fatal, the powdery white coating on your plant looks awful. Remove and destroy any infected plants. Prevent further outbreaks of powdery mildew with a spray of liquid sulfur or a fungicide containing triforine (see pages 145 and 149).

Root Rot

If your flowering tobacco plants wilt suddenly and eventually die, suspect root rot. Dig up and discard infected plants at the first sign of attack; if the problem is root rot, the roots of infected plants will indeed be rotted. Avoid the problem by planting flowering tobacco in a very well drained soil, amended with plenty of compost, leafmold or peat moss. Space plants generously to encourage maximum air circulation.

Tobacco Mosaic Virus

Tobacco mosaic virus causes foliage to become distorted and develop yellow, tan and dark spots. Like most viruses, this one is spread by sucking insects. It may also be spread by gardeners who smoke tobacco and then handle the foliage of flowering tobacco. The only control is to dig up and destroy infected plants at the first sign of attack.

Often grown as a bedding plant, flowering tobacco also makes an excellent container plant. Shown here: 'Domino'.

Paeonia
PEONY

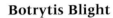

Zones 3–9

Perennial

Anthracnose

Anthracnose is a fungal disease that causes tan or brown spots with purplish black edges to develop on peony foliage. Severely infected plants may become stunted and die. Warm, humid conditions exacerbate the disease. Dig up and destroy any infected plants at the first sign of attack. Avoid overhead watering, space plants generously to increase air circulation, and add an organic mulch to keep disease-infected mud from splashing on peony foliage. To keep the disease from returning, spray with a fungicide containing chlorothalonil; repeat spray every 7 to 10 days (see page 147).

Peony flowers with a single row of petals and a cluster of narrow yellow petals in the center are known as Japanese types; this one is called 'Flame'.

Peonies grow best in regions with cold winters. Plant peonies in a full-sun to partially shaded location in a well-drained garden loam soil. Keep plants evenly moist during the growing season. You may have to stake the heavy flowers to keep them from bending over to the ground.

Botrytis Blight

Botrytis blight (also called gray mold) causes stems and flowers of peonies to rot and possibly become covered with a grayish mold. This fungus is encouraged by periods of cool, humid weather. You can keep the problem from occurring by avoiding overhead watering, incorporating plenty of organic matter into the soil to improve drainage, and by spacing plants generously to increase air circulation. Once the disease strikes, the only solution is to dig up and destroy any infected plants.

Four-Lined Plant Bugs

Four-lined plant bugs cause distorted foliage and flowers, along with yellow to brown spots on leaves. Control both the bugs and their equally destructive nymphs with a spray of insecticidal soap, paying particular attention to the undersides of leaves (see page 144). Repeat spray every three days until the bugs are no longer present.

Japanese Beetles

If you see small holes eaten right through peony leaves, the culprit is likely to be Japanese beetles. The beetles are metallic green or brownish and about $1/2$

inch long. Control with insecticidal soap (see page 144). Control future generations with milky spores which kill the grubs as they overwinter in the soil (see page 150). Chemical controls include products that contain acephate, carbaryl or malathion (see pages 146 and 148).

Oystershell Scale

Scale-infested plants will have bumps on the leaves and stems of plants. The tough outer coating on scale protects the small insect inside, which does damage by sucking plant juices from the stems. If left untreated, the scale will eventually produce a sticky, honeydew secretion which attracts ants and a blackish mildew. If the infestation is not large, simply scrape the scale off the plant using the edge of a dull knife or a plastic scouring pad. Avoid problems with scale by attracting such natural predators as lacewing larvae and beneficial wasps (see page 150).

Leaf Spot

Leaf spot appears on peony foliage as grayish white spots with darker rings. Prevalent during periods of warm, humid weather, you can lessen the effects of this disease by immediately removing and disposing of any infected leaves, avoiding overhead watering and permitting good air circulation between plants with generous spacing.

Phytophthora Blight

Phytophthora blight causes peony foliage to wilt, turn black and die. Blight will eventually affect whole plants. This fungal disease springs up during periods of cool, wet conditions. Dig up and destroy any infected plants at the first sign of attack. To avoid the problem, plant peonies in well-drained soil and space plants generously to increase air circulation. You may be able to stop the spread of this disease by spraying with a fungicide containing mancozeb every 7 to 10 days, especially if the weather turns wet and cool (see page 148).

Root-Knot Nematodes

Root-knot nematodes—microscopic, soil-borne worms—cause stunted growth and yellow foliage. Affected plants eventually die. If you pull up a plant, you'll notice stunted roots with small knots or lumps on them. Dig up and destroy any affected plants. Avoid the problem in the future by solarizing the soil (see page 151) and by incorporating plenty of organic soil amendments into the planting bed.

The product Nematrol has shown some success in controlling root-knot nematodes, as does incorporating chitin into the soil (see page 143).

Slugs and Snails

If you wake up in the morning and find that something has eaten major portions of your peony's new growth—and has left telltale slime

Hybridizers have produced peonies with a wide variety of flower shapes and forms. This is a semi-double form called 'Gay Paree'.

trails—you'll know the culprits are slugs, snails or both. Although there are a number of more-or-less effective natural controls, even the most ardent organic gardeners use a product called Escar-Go, which contains iron phosphate, a naturally occurring soil element (see page 145), to control these frustrating pests. Chemical controls include products (usually in bait form) containing metaldehyde or methiocarb (see page 148). Whether using Escar-Go or a chemical control, scatter it all around potential targets and any damp, shady spot where slugs and snails hide during the day. If you know there are slugs or snails in your area, always treat your garden with a control before their damage is apparent; slugs and snails can do a tremendous amount of damage.

Thrips

Thrips damage appears as silvery or brown spots or streaking on leaves and flowers. Knock thrips off with a strong blast of water. If thrips persist, use an insecticidal soap or azadirachtin (see pages 142 and 144).

Oystershell scale will occasionally attack peonies. See above for more information.

Papaver
POPPY

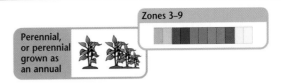
Perennial, or perennial grown as an annual
Zones 3–9

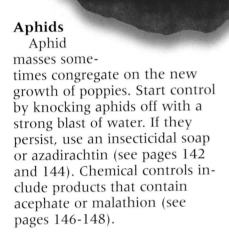

For all their beguiling beauty, poppies are very undemanding plants. They do best in full sun, but are not particular about soil type. They need only occasional watering and no fertilizer. Where adapted, they will readily reseed, returning year after year.

Aphids

Aphid masses sometimes congregate on the new growth of poppies. Start control by knocking aphids off with a strong blast of water. If they persist, use an insecticidal soap or azadirachtin (see pages 142 and 144). Chemical controls include products that contain acephate or malathion (see pages 146-148).

Bacterial Blight

Bacterial blight produces small black spots all over plants, including stems and flowers. Plants eventually turn brown and drop. Dig up and destroy infected plants at the first sign of attack. Avoid overhead watering. To avoid future problems with bacterial blight, solarize the planting bed (see page 151).

Four-Lined Plant Bugs

Four-lined plant bugs cause distorted foliage and flowers, along with yellow to brown spots, to appear on leaves. Control both the bugs and their equally destructive nymphs with a spray of insecticidal soap, paying particular attention to the undersides of leaves (see page 144). Repeat spray every three days until the bugs are no longer present.

Leafhoppers

Small, distorted, yellowish leaves on your poppies are a virus-like culprit known as aster yellows. The malady is spread by aster leafhoppers (also known as the six-spotted leafhopper), so to control the disease you have to control the leafhoppers. Start by picking off any affected growth and disposing of it. Remove the leafhoppers with a strong blast of water, or use an insecticidal soap (see page 144); in either case, be sure to hit both the tops and bottoms of the leaves for complete control. A spray of light horticultural oil will also control leafhoppers by smothering them (see page 144). Chemical controls for leafhoppers include products containing acephate, carbaryl or malathion (see pages 146-148). Make sure poppies are listed on the product label.

Powdery Mildew

Poppies will occasionally be bothered by powdery mildew if growing conditions turn humid. Although the disease is not fatal, the powdery white coating on foliage and flowers is unattractive. Remove and destroy any infected plants. Plant poppies in a full-sun location and space widely to encourage maximum air circulation. Prevent further outbreaks of powdery mildew with a spray of liquid sulfur (see page 145).

Verticillium Wilt

Verticillium wilt causes plants to wilt; at first you may think that the plant needs water, but when it doesn't respond and the foliage turns yellow, you realize the plant is in trouble. Severely infected plants will eventually die. Like most fungal disease, verticillium wilt is exacerbated by periods of cool, wet weather. Heavy, poorly drained soil makes matters worse. Dig up and destroy infected plants at the first sign of attack. Add plenty of organic matter to the soil to improve drainage.

Looking like something from another planet, this spiky pod will open up to reveal the beautiful, brilliant red flower within.

Hybridizing efforts have produced bicolored and double poppies.

Pelargonium
ZONAL GERANIUM

Tender perennial, usually grown as an annual

All Zones

Botrytis Blight

Botrytis blight (also called gray mold) causes stems and flowers of geraniums to rot and to possibly become covered with a grayish mold. This fungus is encouraged by periods of cool, humid weather. Prevent the problem by avoiding overhead watering, incorporating plenty of organic matter into the soil to improve drainage, and by spacing plants generously to increase air circulation. Also, allow soil to dry out slightly between waterings. If the disease does strike, dig up and destroy any infected plants.

Caterpillars

Several caterpillars, including tobacco budworms, cabbage loopers and plume moth caterpillars, eat holes in geranium leaves and flower buds. Natural controls include Bt, Btk and azadirachtin (see pages 142-143). Organic gardeners encourage the presence of the caterpillar's natural enemy, the parasitic wasp, with the wasp's favorite host plants (see page 150). Chemical controls include products containing acephate or carbaryl (see page 146).

Cercospora Leaf Spot

Cercospora leaf spot produces black spots with yellow edges on leaves; over time the affected leaves turn yellow and stems may rot. Leaf spot is spread by water—either rain or from the garden hose—and is most likely to be a problem during wet springs. Remove and discard any damaged leaves (or entire plants) at the first sign of attack. Water early in the day to allow foliage a chance to dry off before nightfall, and avoid overhead watering, to keep the disease from spreading.

Geraniums are hard-working plants that return a lot of pleasure for very little effort. Although they will tolerate light shade, geraniums are best planted in full sun. Plant in a good, well-drained garden loam; allow the soil to dry out somewhat between waterings. Feed geraniums once a year about midway through the growing season.

Chemical controls include products containing copper sulfate or streptomycin. After pruning affected foliage, dip shears in rubbing alcohol to disinfect them.

Geraniums, and their close cousins perlargoniums, are available in shades of red, pink, coral, lavender and white. Shown here: 'Freckles'.

notice mealybugs on the foliage, start control by knocking them off with a strong blast of water. If the infestation continues, spray with an insecticidal soap, paying special attention to the undersides of leaves (see page 144). Chemical controls include products containing malathion or carbaryl (see pages 146-148).

Rust

If there are yellow spots on geranium leaves, with powdery orange-brown spots on the undersides of the foliage, the plants have become infected with rust. Spread by the wind, rust is best controlled by removing any infected foliage (or whole plants) as soon as the disease makes an appearance. To prevent further problems, spray plants with a sulfur mixture (see page 145).

Geranium Aphids

Small tan, green or black geranium aphids sometimes congregate on new growth. Start control by knocking aphids off with a strong blast of water. If they persist, use an insecticidal soap or azadirachtin (see pages 142 and 144). A spray of light horticultural oil will control aphids by smothering them (see page 144). Chemical controls include products that contain acephate or malathion (see pages 146-148).

Leafrollers and Leaftiers

If individual geranium leaves are folded or rolled, with or without fine webbing, the problem is leafrollers or leaftiers. Unroll one of the leaves and you'll probably catch the culprits in action: small green, brown or yellow caterpillars. Pick off and discard any affected leaves. Control with sprays is difficult because the caterpillars are protected by the rolled or folded leaves. Chemical controls include products containing acephate or carbaryl (see page 146).

Mealybugs

You'll definitely know if your geraniums have mealybugs: their distinctive fuzzy white bodies (about $1/4$ inch long) look like nothing else in the pest world. If you

Pelargonium rust shows up as small, rust-colored spots on the undersides of leaves. Pick off and destroy any infected leaves; see above for further controls.

Slugs and Snails

If something has eaten major portions of your geranium's new growth—and has left telltale slime trails—you'll know the culprits are slugs, snails or both. Escar-Go, which contains iron phosphate, a naturally occurring soil element (see page 145), seems to control these frustrating pests. Chemical controls include products (usually in bait form) containing metaldehyde or methiocarb (see page 148). Whether using Escar-Go or a chemical control, scatter it all around potential targets and any damp, shady spot where slugs and snails hide during the day. If you know there are slugs or snails in your area, always treat your garden with a control before their damage is apparent; slugs and snails can do a tremendous amount of damage in even one night.

Southern Root-Knot Nematodes

Microscopic, soil-borne southern root-knot nematodes cause stunted growth and yellow foliage. Affected plants eventually die. If you pull up a plant, you'll notice stunted roots with small knots or lumps on them. Dig up and destroy any affected plants. Solarize the soil (see page 151) to avoid future problems, and incorporate plenty of organic soil amendments into the planting bed. The product Nematrol has shown some success in controlling southern root-knot nematodes, as does incorporating chitin (see page 143) into the soil.

Spider Mites

Spider mites can attack geraniums, especially during periods of hot, dry weather. Telltale damage includes stippled, grayish foliage and stunted growth. The mites attack the undersides of leaves and usually leave small holes and fine webbing in their wake. Blast mites off with a strong spray of water, paying particular attention to the undersides of the leaves. If the problem persists, use an insecticidal soap (see page 144) or smother the mites with a spray of light horticultural oil. If infestation is heavy, spray with a specially formulated miticide containing hexakis (see page 148).

Whiteflies

If your geranium plants are lacking in vigor, are pale, and if clouds of very small white insects fly up when the leaves are disturbed, you've got whitefly infestation. To control, use an insecticidal soap, azadirachtin, or smother the pests with a spray of light horticultural oil; pay special attention to the leaves' undersides (see page 144). Or simply blast the whiteflies off the plants with a strong spray of water.

Viruses

If your geranium plants or flowers are stunted with mottled, streaked or unusually colored foliage, the problem is a virus. Since there is no cure for viral diseases, dig up and destroy any infected plants at the first sign of attack. To help avoid viral diseases, control insects such as aphids and leafhoppers, which spread viruses as they suck on plants. A spray of insecticidal soap will control both aphids and leafhoppers (see page 144).

Geranium 'Showcase Pink Parfait'.

Penstemon
PENSTEMON

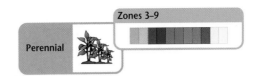

Perennial

Zones 3–9

The penstemon family is a huge one and includes many wonderful flowering perennials. They do best in a full sun location but tolerate light shade. Plant in a very well-drained soil and allow plants to dry out somewhat between waterings. These are lean plants, requiring no fertilizer.

Aphids

Aphids sometimes congregate on the new growth of penstemon. Start control by knocking aphids off with a strong blast of water. If they persist, use an insecticidal soap or azadirachtin (see pages 142 and 144). Chemical controls include products that contain acephate or malathion (see pages 146-149).

Leaf Spot

Leaf spot appears on penstemon foliage as yellow, brown or purplish black spots, especially during periods of warm, humid weather; you can lessen this disease by immediately removing and disposing of any infected leaves, avoiding overhead watering, and permitting good air circulation between plants with generous spacing. Avoid future damage from leaf spot with a sulfur spray (see page 145).

Rust

If there are yellow spots on penstemon leaves, with powdery orange-brown spots on the undersides of the foliage, the plants are infected with the disease known as rust, which is spread by the wind. The best control is to remove any infected foliage (or whole plants) as soon as the disease makes an appearance and to avoid overhead watering. To prevent further problems, spray plants with a sulfur mixture (see page 145).

Southern Blight

In warm, humid growing climates southern blight (also known as crown rot) may create problems for penstemons. This disease causes whole plants to rot at soil level and die. Telltale signs of crown rot are white, threadlike formations at the base of the penstemon. About the only control is to dig up and discard infected plants.

Tobacco Budworms

Tobacco budworms are typical chewing caterpillars of a night-flying moth. Their damage includes small holes in flowers and buds. Control with a spray of Btk (*Bacillus thuringiensis* var. *kurstaki*) or an insecticide containing acephate or carbaryl (see pages 143 and 146). Repeat spray every 10 to 14 days until the caterpillars are no longer present.

Penstemon gloxinioides *'Midnight'*, one of the many blue- to purple-flowered penstemons.

Petunia
PETUNIA

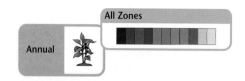

Annual · All Zones

The intensely pink 'Polo' petunia.

Petunias do best in a full-sun location, planted in a good garden loam. Keep soil consistently moist but not wet. Feed monthly with a complete fertilizer.

Bacterial Fasciation

This strange disease is caused by soil-borne bacteria and produces wide, flattened stems—as if several plants have been fused together. Dig up and destroy any infected plants. Avoid the problem in the future by solarizing the planting bed (see page 151).

Caterpillars

Two caterpillars—tobacco budworms and yellow woollybear caterpillars—eat holes in petunia leaves and flower buds. Natural controls include Bt and azadirachtin (see pages 142-143). Chemical controls include products containing acephate or carbaryl (see page 146).

Colorado Potato Beetles

Colorado potato beetles and their larvae are voracious eaters and can defoliate petunia plants in a hurry. Avoid the problem in the future by ridding the garden beds of all garden debris each fall. A spray of Btsd (*Bacillus thuringiensis* var. *san diego*) will kill the beetle nymphs and grubs (see page 143). Other controls include insecticides containing pyrethrin, rotenone, azadirachtin or carbaryl (see pages 142-149).

Cucumber mosaic virus

Cucumber mosaic virus is spread by sucking insects and causes distorted foliage speckled with yellow and a reduction of flowers. Dig up and destroy infected plants at the first sign of attack. Avoid problems in the future by controlling aphids and other sucking insects with a spray of insecticidal soap (see page 144).

Dodder

There's no mistaking dodder with any other malady: You'll notice thin, orange strands woven about the petunia plants. These strands are actually parasitic plants, sucking the nutrition from the host. Dig up and destroy any infected plants at the first sign of attack. There is no known cure for this parasitic pest.

Potato Flea Beetles

Potato flea beetles are very small, shiny black beetles that produce small holes ($1/8$-inch) in the leaves of petunias. The beetles jump around like fleas. Affected foliage may wilt and eventually die. Control with a spray of insecticidal soap (see page 144). Other controls include insecticides containing pyrethrin, carbaryl or methoxychlor (see pages 142-149).

Slugs and Snails

If you wake up in the morning and find that something has eaten major portions of your petunia's new growth—and has left telltale slime trails—you'll know the culprits are slugs, snails or both. Although there are a number of more-or-less ef-

The aptly named 'Joy Star' petunia.

fective natural controls, even the most ardent organic gardeners have begun using a product called Escar-Go, which contains iron phosphate, a naturally occurring soil element (see page 145), to control these frustrating pests. Chemical controls include products (usually in bait form) containing metaldehyde or methiocarb (see page 148). Scatter Escar-Go or a chemical control all around potential targets and any damp, shady spot where slugs and snails hide during the day. If you know there are slugs or snails in your area, always treat your garden with a control before their damage is apparent; slugs and snails can do a tremendous amount of damage in even one night.

Spotted

It took hybridizers many years to find the key to producing a yellow petunia. Shown here: 'Summer Sun'.

Cucumber Beetles

Spotted cucumber beetles munch on petunia leaves and flowers, leaving holes or ragged edges. The beetles themselves are about $1/4$ inch long, yellowish green in color, with black spots. Beneficial nematodes will help prevent spotted cucumber beetle as will an application of milky spores (*Bacillus popilliae* and *B. lentimorbus*); see page 143. Chemical controls include products which contain carbaryl or pyrethrins (see pages 146-149).

Southern Root-Knot Nematodes

Southern root-knot Nematodes—microscopic, soil-borne worms—cause stunted growth and yellow foliage. Affected plants eventually die. If you pull up a plant, you'll find stunted roots with small knots or lumps. Dig up and destroy any affected plants. To avoid the problem in the future: Solarize the soil (see page 151) and incorporate plenty of organic soil amendments. Nematrol has shown some success in controlling southern root-knot nematodes, as does incorporating chitin into the soil (see page 143).

Planted in a limited color range, free-flowering petunias make a big impact.

Phlox
PHLOX

Annuals and perennials

Annuals: All Zones

Perennials: Zones 3–9

Nematodes

Nematodes—microscopic, soil-borne worms—cause stunted growth and yellow foliage. Affected plants eventually die. If you pull up a plant, you'll notice stunted roots with small knots or lumps on them. Dig up and destroy any affected plants. Avoid the problem in the future by solarizing the soil (see page 151) and incorporating plenty of organic soil amendments into the planting bed. Nematrol has shown some success in controlling nematodes, as does incorporating chitin into the soil (see page 143).

Powdery Mildew

Phlox is known as being very susceptible to powdery mildew, especially if growing conditions turn humid. Although the disease is not fatal, its signature powdery white coating on foliage and flowers is unattractive.

Remove and destroy any infected plants. Prevent further outbreaks of powdery mildew with a spray of light horticultural oil (see page 144). Avoid the problem altogether by planting mildew-resistant varieties of phlox (see page 21).

Phlox Plant Bugs

Phlox plant bugs cause phlox foliage and flowers to become deformed or stunted; light-colored spots may appear on new growth. Both the phlox plant bugs and their nymphs cause damage. Control with a spray of insecticidal soap, light horticultural oil (which will smother the pests), or with azadirachtin (see page 142).

Spider Mites

Spider mites can attack phlox, especially during periods of hot, dry weather. Telltale damage includes stippled, grayish foliage and stunted growth. The mites attack the undersides of leaves and usually leave small holes and fine webbing in their wake. Blast mites off with a strong spray of water. If the problem persists, use an insecticidal soap or a spray of light horticultural oil which will smother the pests (see page 144). With any spray (including water), pay special attention to the undersides of leaves. If infestation is severe, spray with a specially formulated miticide containing hexakis (see page 148).

Southern Blight

In warm, humid growing climates, southern blight (also known as crown rot) may create problems for phlox. This disease causes whole plants to rot at soil level and die. Telltale signs of crown rot are white, threadlike formations at the base of the plants. About the only control is to dig up and discard infected plants. To avoid problems in the future, incorporate plenty of organic matter into the soil; this will improve drainage.

An old-fashioned favorite, phlox does best in a full-sun location, planted in a well-drained garden loam; feed once, about midway through the growing season, with a complete fertilizer.

Rosa
ROSE

Woody shrub

Zones 3–9

Whatever effort they demand, roses pay it back hand-somely. Almost all roses do best in a full-sun location with good air circulation. They should be planted in a well-drained garden loam and fed monthly with a complete fertilizer during the growing season. The little work they actually require produces beauties like this fully open blossom of 'Elinor le Grice'.

Aphids

Aphids (masses of small tan, green or black insects) commonly congregate on the new growth of roses. To start, knock aphids off with a strong blast of water. If they persist, use an insecticidal soap or azadirachtin (see pages 142 and 144). Chemical controls include products that contain acephate or malathion (see pages 146-148).

Bristly Rose Slugs

Bristly rose slugs are the slug-like larvae of the sawfly. They're hungry feeders, leaving large, chewed holes in leaves; some leaves may be devoured to the point where only a skeleton is left. Control with a spray of insecticidal soap (see page 144).

Brown Canker

Brown canker produces dark, purplish spots on rose canes. This fungal disease infects roses through wounds in the canes of the plants. Leave damage until it's time for winter pruning, then prune canes six inches or so below any infected spots. Destroy infected prunings; do not compost. Clean pruners with rubbing alcohol between prunings. To prevent future infection, spray roses with Bordeaux mix while dormant (see page 143).

Black Spot

Black spot, just as the name implies, shows up as black spots on rose foliage and canes. This fungal disease is a particular problem during periods of warm, wet weather. Start control by pruning off and destroying any infected foliage or canes. Spray with liquid sulfur or baking soda mixture (see pages 143 and 145). Avoid future problems by giving roses enough room around them to provide good air circulation, and *do not wet* foliage when watering. Or sidestep the problem altogether by planting rose varieties resistant to black spot (see page 21).

If you catch an infestation of aphids at the first sign of attack, you'll be able to get rid of them with a strong blast of water.

The hybrid musk rose 'Efurt'.

Climbing roses put on a show unlike any other climbing or vining plant.

and rose budworms, eat holes in rose leaves and flower buds; fine webbing may be present near areas of damage. Natural controls include Bt (*Bacillus thuringiensis*) and azadirachtin (see pages 142-143). Organic gardeners encourage the presence of the caterpillar's natural enemy, the parasitic wasp, with the wasp's favorite host plants (see page 150). Chemical controls include products containing acephate or carbaryl (see page 146).

Japanese Beetles

If you see small holes eaten right through rose foliage, the culprit is likely to be Japanese beetles. The beetles are metallic green or brownish and about $1/2$ inch long. Control with insecticidal soap (see page 144). Control future generations with milky disease spores; these kill the grubs as they overwinter in the soil (see page 150). Chemical controls include products that contain acephate, carbaryl or malathion (see pages 146 and 148).

Borers

Borers, as their name suggests, bore holes in the main stems of plants and live inside, eating the plants from the inside out. If sections of plants suddenly wilt, despite sufficient water, check for telltale small holes in the stems surrounded by a fine sawdust-like material called frass. About all you can do is dig up and destroy any infected plants or portions of plants.

Botrytis Blight

Botrytis blight (also called gray mold) causes stems and flowers of roses to rot and possibly become covered with a grayish mold. This fungus is encouraged by periods of cool, humid weather. Keep the problem from occurring by avoiding overhead watering, incorporating plenty of organic matter into the soil to improve drainage, and by spacing plants generously to increase air circulation. Once the disease strikes, you'll just have to dig up and destroy any infected plants.

Fuller Rose Beetles

Fuller rose beetles are frustrating pests; they not only greedily chew rose foliage, but they also make holes in flower buds, which then may not open. Prune off and destroy any infected foliage and flower buds. Avoid future problems with an application of beneficial nematodes; apply while pests are present (see page 150).

Caterpillars

Several caterpillars, including fall webworms

Powdery Mildew

Powdery mildew may become a problem on roses, especially if growing conditions turn humid. Although the disease is not fatal, the powdery white coating on foliage and flowers is unattractive. Remove and destroy any infected plants.

With their long season of bloom, long sturdy stems for cutting and fabulous colors, hybrid tea roses, like these, have been favorites of home gardeners for years.

Prevent further outbreaks of powdery mildew with a spray of liquid sulfur or baking soda (see pages 143 and 145).

Rose Midges

These tiny white maggots cause rose buds and new growth to turn black and shrivel. About the only control: Prune off and destroy all infected parts.

Rust

If rose foliage shows yellow or darkish spots on top and powdery orange-brown spots underneath, the plants are suffering from rust, which is spread by the wind; the best control is to remove any infected foliage as soon as the disease makes an appearance. To prevent further problems, spray plants with a sulfur spray (see page 145).

Scale

Scale-infested plants will have gray or light-colored bumps on the leaves and stems of plants. The tough outer coating on scale protects the small insect inside, which does damage by sucking plant juices from the stems. If left untreated, the scale will eventually produce a sticky,

Red remains the home gardener's favorite rose color.

honeydew secretion which attracts ants and a blackish mildew. If the infestation is not large, simply scrape the scale off the plant using the edge of a dull knife or a plastic scouring pad. Avoid problems with scale by attracting such natural predators as lacewing larvae and beneficial wasps (see page 150).

Spider Mites

Spider mites can attack roses, especially during periods of hot, dry weather. Damage includes stippled, grayish foliage and stunted growth. The mites attack the undersides of leaves and usually leave small holes and fine webbing in their wake. Blast mites off with a strong spray of water; pay attention to the undersides of the leaves. If the problem persists,

use an insecticidal soap or smother the pests with a spray of light horticultural oil (see page 144). If infestation is severe, spray with a specially formulated miticide containing hexakis (see page 148).

Thrips

Thrips damage appears as silvery or brown spots or streaking on leaves and flowers. Start by knocking thrips off with a strong blast of water. If thrips persist, use an insecticidal soap or azadirachtin (see pages 142 and 144).

Viruses

If the flowers on your roses are stunted with mottled, streaked or unusually colored foliage, the problem is a virus. As there is no cure for viral diseases, dig up and destroy any infected plants at the first sign of attack. Help avoid virus diseases by controlling insects (such as aphids and leafhoppers) which spread viruses as they suck on plants. A spray of insecticidal soap will control both aphids and leafhoppers (see page 144).

The floribunda rose 'Tabris'.

The shrub rose 'Robusta'.

Rudbeckia
BLACK-EYED SUSAN

Annual, biennial, or perennial

Annuals & Biennials: All Zones

Perennials: Zones 3–9

Brown Ambrosia Aphids

Brown ambrosia aphids cause stunted new growth on black-eyed Susans. The evidence: a shiny black coating on the plants. Start control by knocking aphids off with a strong blast of water. If they persist, use an insecticidal soap or azadirachtin (see pages 142 and 144). Chemical controls include products that contain acephate or malathion (see pages 146-148).

Leafhoppers

If you notice small, distorted, yellowish leaves on your black-eyed Susans, the problem is a virus-like culprit known as aster yellows. The problem is spread by aster leafhoppers (also known as the six-spotted leafhopper); so to control aster yellows, you have to control the leafhoppers. Start by picking off any affected growth and disposing of it. The leafhoppers can be removed with a strong blast of water, or by using an insecticidal soap (see page 144); in either case, be sure to hit both the tops and bottoms of the leaves. Chemical controls for leafhoppers include products containing acephate, carbaryl or malathion (see pages 146-148). Make sure black-eyed Susans are listed on the product label.

Powdery Mildew

Black-eyed Susans will occasionally be bothered by powdery mildew if growing conditions turn humid. Although the disease is not fatal, its powdery white coating on foliage and flowers looks bad. Remove and destroy any infected plants. Prevent further outbreaks of powdery mildew with a spray of liquid sulfur, light horticultural oil or baking soda (see pages 143-144).

Rust

If black-eyed Susans show powdery orange-brown spots on the undersides of leaves, the plants have become infected with the disease known as rust. Spread by the wind, rust is best controlled by removing any infected foliage (or whole plants) as soon as the disease makes an appearance. To prevent further problems, spray plants with a sulfur mixture (see page 145).

Black-eyed Susans are among the easiest of all perennials to grow. The only thing they won't tolerate is poorly drained, soggy soil. Plant in a full sun location, in any type of soil; allow to dry out somewhat between waterings. Black-eyed Susans do not require fertilizer.

Sedum
SEDUM

Perennial

Zones 3–9

Plant sedums in a full-sun location, in a good garden loam with excellent drainage. Allow them to dry out somewhat between waterings; feed once, about midway through the growing season, with a complete fertilizer. Shown here: the deservedly popular 'Autumn Joy'.

Aphids

Aphids, those masses of small tan, green or black insects, sometimes congregate on the new sedum growth. Start control by knocking aphids off with a strong blast of water. If they persist, use an insecticidal soap or azadirachtin (see pages 142 and 144). Chemical controls include products that contain acephate or malathion (see pages 146-148).

Root Rot

If you notice the base of your sedum plants rotting and turning black, the problem is root rot. Dig up and discard infected plants at the first sign of attack. Avoid the problem by planting sedums in a very well drained soil, amended with plenty of compost, leafmold or peat moss.

Rust

If your sedums show powdery orange-brown spots on the undersides of leaves, with yellow or darkish spots on top, the plants have become infected with rust. Spread by the wind, rust is best controlled by removing any infected foliage (or whole plants) as soon as the disease makes an appearance. To prevent further problems, spray plants with a sulfur mixture (see page 145).

Scale

Scale infested plants will have gray or light-colored bumps on the leaves and stems of plants. The tough outer coating on scale protects the small insect inside, which does damage by sucking plant juices from the stems. If left untreated, the scale will eventually produce a sticky, honeydew secretion which attracts ants and a blackish fungus. If the infestation is not large, simply scrape the scale off the plant using the edge of a dull knife or a plastic scouring pad. Avoid problems with scale by attracting such natural predators as lacewing larvae and beneficial wasps.

Southern Blight

Southern blight causes thin webbing to appear at the bases of the plants and on top of nearby soil; sedum stems may rot and turn black at soil level and the foliage may turn yellow. This fungal disease thrives in warm climates and moist soils low in nitrogen. Dig up and destroy all infected plants at the first sign of attack. Remove and discard any soil that the roots have touched. About the only way to avoid problems from southern blight in the future is to solarize the planting beds (see page 151).

Senecio
DUSTY MILLER

Perennial, usually grown as an annual

All Zones

Powdery Mildew

Dusty miller will occasionally be bothered by powdery mildew if growing conditions turn humid. Although the disease is not fatal, its signature powdery white coating on foliage and flowers is very unattractive. Remove and destroy any infected plants.

Prevent further outbreaks of powdery mildew with a spray of liquid sulfur (see page 145).

Rust

If your dusty millers show powdery orange-brown spots on the undersides of leaves, and the leaves have yellow or darkish spots on top, the plants have become infected with the disease known as rust. Spread by the wind, rust is best controlled by removing any infected foliage (or whole plants) as soon as the disease makes an appearance. To prevent further problems, spray plants with a sulfur mixture (see page 145).

Southern Blight

In warm, humid growing climates southern blight (also known as crown rot) may create problems for dusty miller. This disease causes whole plants to rot at soil level and die. Telltale signs of crown rot are white, threadlike formations at the base of the plant. About the only control: Dig up and discard infected plants. To avoid problems in the future, incorporate plenty of organic matter into the soil to improve drainage. Avoid future problems with southern blight by solarizing the soil (see page 151).

Dusty miller, and other forms of senecio, are easy-to-grow plants with wonderful gray or silver foliage. Choose a full-sun location and water sparingly. Dusty miller is tolerant of a wide variety of soils, as long as it's well drained; no fertilizer is required.

Dusty miller (S. cineraria)—a close relative of bachelor's buttons—is valued for its silver foliage.

Tagetes
MARIGOLD

Annual   All Zones

Aphids

Aphids sometimes congregate on the new growth of marigolds; knock them off with a strong blast of water. If they persist, use an insecticidal soap or azadirachtin (see pages 142 and 144). Chemical controls include products that contain acephate or malathion (see pages 146-148).

Aster Yellows

Aster yellows, a virus-like disease, occasionally attacks marigolds. Affected leaves will be weakened and have a mottled yellow appearance. Since there is no cure for this disease, simply remove and destroy any affected plants. Wash hands with soap and hot water after touching foliage affected with aster yellows, because the disease can be spread by simply touching other leaves and flowers. If you use pruning shears to cut out affected foliage, dip the blades in rubbing alcohol after use to disinfect them. Avoid future problems by controlling aster leafhoppers (which spread the disease) with a spray of insecticidal soap (see page 144).

Botrytis Blight

Botrytis blight (also called gray mold) causes brown blotches on marigold foliage and possibly covers it with a grayish mold. Periods of cool, humid weather encourage this fungus. You can keep the problem from occurring by avoiding overhead watering, incorporating plenty of organic matter into the soil to improve drainage, and by spacing plants generously to increase air circulation. Once the disease does strike, the only solution is to dig up and destroy any infected plants.

European Earwigs

European earwigs will sometimes nibble on new marigold growth, leaving partially eaten leaves in their wake. Nightfeeders, earwigs retreat to cool, dark places during the day. The easiest way to control them is to make a few traps of damp, rolled-up newspaper; during the day, the earwigs will crawl into the traps, which then can simply be thrown away. If you have a serious infestation of earwigs, there are specially formulated earwig baits that are effective controls.

One of the workhorses of the summer flower garden, marigolds do their blooming job well and with very little help from the gardener. All they require is a full-sun location, a well drained garden loam, regular watering and a once-a-month feeding with a complete fertilizer. Shown here: 'Mighty Marietta'.

Japanese Beetles

If you see small holes eaten right through marigold leaves, the culprit is likely to be Japanese beetles. They are metallic green or brownish and about $^1/_2$ inch long. Control with insecticidal soap (see page 144). Control future generations with milky disease spores which kill the grubs as they overwinter in the soil (see page 150). Chemical controls include products that contain acephate, carbaryl or malathion (see pages 146 and 148).

Leafrollers and Leaftiers

If individual marigold leaves are folded or rolled, with or without fine webbing, the problem is leafrollers or leaftiers. Unroll one of the leaves and you'll probably catch the culprits in action: small green, brown or yellow caterpillars. Pick off and discard any affected leaves. Control with sprays is difficult because the caterpillars are protected by the rolled or folded leaves. Chemical controls include products containing acephate or carbaryl (see page 146).

Leafhoppers

If you notice aster yellows on your marigolds, you probably have leafhoppers as well. The problem is spread by aster leafhoppers (also known as six-spotted leafhoppers), so to control aster yellows, you have to control the leafhoppers. Start by picking off any affected growth and disposing of it. The leafhoppers can be removed with a strong blast of water, by using an insecticidal soap, or by smothering the pests with a light horticultural oil (see page 144); in any case, be sure to hit both the tops and bottoms of the leaves for complete control. Chemical controls for leafhoppers include products containing acephate, carbaryl or malathion (see pages 146-148). Make sure marigolds are listed on the product label.

Slugs and Snails

If something eats major portions (or *all*) of your marigold's new growth—and has left telltale slime trails—you'll know you have slugs, snails or both. Although there are a number of more-or-less effective natural controls, even the most ardent organic gardeners have begun using a product called Escar-Go, which contains iron phosphate, a naturally occurring soil element (see page 145), to control these frustrating pests. Chemical controls include products (usually in bait form) containing metaldehyde or methiocarb (see page 148). Whether using Escar-Go or a chemical control, scatter it all around potential targets and any damp, shady spot where slugs and snails hide during the day. If you know there are slugs or snails in your area, always treat your garden with a control before their damage is apparent; slugs and snails can do a tremendous amount of damage in even one night.

Spider Mites

Spider mites can attack marigolds, especially during periods of hot, dry weather. Telltale damage includes stippled, grayish foliage and stunted growth. The mites attack the undersides of leaves and usually leave small holes and fine webbing in their wake. Blast mites off with a strong spray of water, paying particular attention to the undersides of the leaves. If the problem persists, use an insecticidal soap or smother the pests with a spray of light horticultural oil (see page 144). If infestation is severe, spray with a specially formulated miticide containing hexakis (see page 148).

Southern Blight

In warm, humid growing climates southern blight (also known as crown rot) may create problems for marigolds. This disease causes whole plants to rot at soil level and die. Signs of crown rot are white, threadlike formations at the base of the plant. The only control is to dig up and discard infected plants. To avoid future problems, solarize the soil (see page 151).

Tarnished Plant Bugs

Tarnished plant bugs are most active in the early spring but may persist through summer. As they feed on foliage, they inject toxins into the plant which results in deformed foliage and flowers, which may eventually turn black. Control tarnished plant bugs with a spray of insecticidal soap (see page 144).

Wilt and Stem Rot

Wilt and stem rot causes the stems of marigolds to turn black at their bases, possibly with a covering of mold. Foliage will turn yellow; plants eventually fall over and die. Begin control by digging up and destroying any infected plants. Avoid the problem in the future by improving soil drainage with the incorporation of plenty of organic matter. If you use a mulch, keep it an inch or so away from the stems of the plants and allow the soil to dry out slightly between waterings.

Tall-growing marigolds, perfect for use in bouquets, peek out between these pickets.

Tropaeolum
NASTURTIUM

With their willingness to grow, nasturtiums are very satsifying plants. Provide them with a full-sun to light-shade location. Nasturtiums do best in very well drained, or sandy soils; keep the soil evenly moist through the growing season.

Bacterial Wilt

If your nasturtiums suddenly wilt, even though there's sufficient moisture in the soil, bacterial wilt is the probable cause—especially if there's been an extended period of warm weather. Dig up and destroy any infected plants at the first sign of attack. Remove all soil touched by the roots. To avoid problems in the future, incorporate plenty of organic matter into the planting bed, and keep the beds free of garden debris. Maximize air circulation: Don't overcrowd plants.

Bean Aphids

Aphids—masses of small green or black insects—sometimes congregate on the new growth of nasturtiums. Start control by knocking aphids off with a strong blast of water. If they persist, use an insecticidal soap or azadirachtin (see pages 142 and 144). Chemical controls include products that contain acephate or malathion (see pages 146-149).

Caterpillars

Two caterpillars in particular—cabbage loopers and imported cabbageworms—eat holes in nasturtium leaves and flower buds. Natural controls include Btk (*Bacillus thuringiensis* var. *kurstaki*), and azadirachtin (see pages 142-143). Organic gardeners encourage the presence of the caterpillar's natural enemy, the parasitic wasp, with the wasp's favorite host plants (see page 150). Chemical controls include products containing acephate or carbaryl (see page 146).

Potato Flea Beetles

Potato flea beetles are very small, shiny black beetles that produce small holes (1/8-inch) in the leaves of nasturtiums. The beetles jump around like fleas when disturbed. Affected foliage may wilt and eventually die. Control with a spray of insecticidal soap (see page 144). Other controls include insecticides containing pyrethrin, carbaryl or methoxychlor (see pages 146-149).

Serpentine Leafminers

Serpentine leafminers are the very small larvae of a tiny fly. The larvae mine their way into the leaves, producing characteristic serpentine, tan-colored trails on the foliage. Prune off and destroy any affected foliage. Avoid future problems with leafminers by applying beneficial nematodes to the soil (see page 150).

Cheery nasturtium flowers make good cut flowers; just reach down into the foliage to cut the longest possible stems. Shown here: 'Whirlybird'.

Tulipa
TULIP

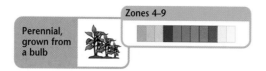

Perennial, grown from a bulb

Zones 4–9

Aphids

Aphids can congregate on the new growth of tulips. To start, knock them off with a strong blast of water. If they persist, use an insecticidal soap or azadirachtin (see pages 142 and 144). Chemical controls include products that contain acephate or malathion (see pages 146-148).

Bulb Mites

Bulb mites are very small insects that burrow into tulip bulbs, transmitting diseases that either keep the bulbs from sprouting or cause them to have yellow foliage. Tulip bulbs infected with mites may rot in storage. Dispose of any soft or rotting bulbs immediately. Control bulb mites by attracting their natural predators with such plants as alyssum and scabiosa.

Cucumber Mosaic Virus

This viral disease is spread by sucking insects, especially aphids. Infected plants will have yellow- and brown-colored streaks in the leaves, may be distorted, and possibly wilt suddenly. Control sucking insects with a spray of insecticidal soap (see page 144). Dig up and destroy any infected bulbs. Do not grow tulips near cucumber plants or gladiolus, both of which harbor the virus.

Tulip Breaking Virus

Tulip breaking virus produces pale streaks in leaves; flower petals may be streaked with light colors as well. Extreme infections cause lower leaves to turn yellow. Dig up and destroy any infected bulbs at the first sign of attack. Like other viruses, this one is spread by sucking insects (such as aphids). While the disease is incurable, use a spray of insecticidal soap to stop the insects from spreading it further (see page 144).

Two-Spotted Spider Mites

Unusually pale leaves, spotted with tiny white or yellow dots, sometimes with fine web-

Darwin tulips, with their wonderful form and brilliant colors.

bing, mean two-spotted spider mites have invaded your tulips. To start control, knock the mites off with a strong blast of water. Use an insecticidal soap for additional control (see page 144). Chemical controls include miticides that include the active ingredient hexakis (see page 148).

Tulips are the prize of many a spring garden. Available in a wondrous array of colors and forms, when it comes to tulips, there is truly something for everyone. Plant in a full-sun location in a well-drained garden loam. Keep the soil evenly moist, but not soggy, up until blooming time. After blooming, allow soil to dry out somewhat between waterings. Allow foliage to die naturally after blooming. Shown here: 'White Triumphator'.

Verbena
VERBENA

Zones 7–9

Perennial, often grown as an annual

Intensely-colored verbena makes a great groundcover, especially if you can provide it with the full-sun, high-heat location it thrives in. Plant in a very well drained garden loam and allow the soil to dry out somewhat between waterings.

Aphids

Aphids sometimes congregate on the new growth of verbena. Start control by knocking aphids off with a strong blast of water. If they persist, use an insecticidal soap or azadirachtin (see pages 142 and 144). Chemical controls include products that contain acephate or malathion (see pages 146-148).

Powdery Mildew

Verbena will occasionally be bothered by powdery mildew if growing conditions turn humid. Although the disease is not fatal, its signature powdery white coating on foliage and flowers is unattractive. Remove and destroy any infected plants. Prevent further outbreaks of powdery mildew with a spray of liquid sulfur or baking soda (see pages 143 and 145).

Spider Mites

Spider mites can attack verbena, especially during periods of hot, dry weather. Telltale damage includes stippled, grayish foliage and stunted growth. The mites attack the undersides of leaves and usually leave small holes and fine webbing in their wake. Blast mites off with a strong spray of water, paying particular attention to the undersides of the leaves. If the problem persists, use an insecticidal soap or smother the pests with a spray of light horticultural oil (see page 144). If infestation is severe, spray with a specially formulated miticide containing hexakis (see page 148).

Verbena Leafminers

Verbena leafminers are the very small larvae of a tiny fly. These larvae mine their way into the leaves, producing serpentine, tan-colored trails on the foliage. Prune off and destroy any affected foliage. To avoid future problems with leafminers, apply beneficial nematodes to the soil (see page 150).

Whiteflies

If your verbena plants are lacking in vigor, are pale, and if clouds of very small white insects fly up when the leaves are disturbed, you've got an infestation of whiteflies. To control, use an insecticidal soap, azadirachtin, or smother the pests with a spray of light horticultural oil (see page 144); or simply blast the whiteflies off the plants with a strong spray of water.

Veronica
VERONICA

Perennial

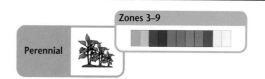

Zones 3–9

Veronica does best in a full-sun location. Plant in a good garden loam and keep the soil consistently damp, but not wet.

Chalcedon Checkerspot Butterflies

The larvae of these butterflies like to chew holes in veronica leaves, sometimes leaving fine webbing behind. Control with a spray of Btk (*Bacillus thuringiensis* var. *kurstaki*); see page 143.

Downy Mildew

Veronica will occasionally be bothered by downy mildew, especially if growing conditions become cool and damp. Although the disease is not fatal, the light-colored patches that appear on the tops of leaves are unattractive, as is the mold that may appear on the underside of foliage. Remove and destroy any infected foliage. Space plants generously to increase air circulation. Prevent further outbreaks of downy mildew with a spray of fixed copper (see page 143).

Foxglove Aphids

Foxglove aphids, those masses of small tan, green or black insects, sometimes congregate on the new growth of veronica. Start control by knocking aphids off with a strong blast of water. If they persist, use an insecticidal soap or azadirachtin (see pages 142 and 144). Chemical controls include products that contain acephate or malathion (see pages 146-148).

Leaf Spot

Leaf spot appears on veronica foliage as yellow spots that gradually darken. Prevalent during periods of warm, humid weather, this disease can be lessened by immediately removing and disposing of any infected leaves, avoiding overhead watering, and permitting good air circulation between plants with generous spacing.

Powdery Mildew

Veronica will occasionally be bothered by powdery mildew if growing conditions turn humid. Although the disease is not fatal, the powdery white coating it produces on foliage and flowers is unattractive. Remove and destroy any infected plants. Prevent further outbreaks of powdery mildew with a spray of liquid sulfur or baking soda (see pages 143 and 145).

Rust

If veronica leaves show powdery, orange-brown spots, the plants have become infected with the disease known as rust. Spread by the wind, rust is best controlled by removing any infected foliage (or whole plants) as soon as the disease makes an appearance. To prevent further problems, spray plants with a sulfur mixture (see page 145).

Viola
PANSY

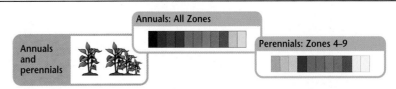

Annuals and perennials

Annuals: All Zones

Perennials: Zones 4–9

Leaf Spot

Leaf spot appears on pansy foliage as various-colored spots

Pansies and violas are old-fashioned flowers few can resist. They prefer growing during the cooler months of spring and fade somewhat during the heat of summer. Plant in full sun in cool parts of the country; in partial shade in hotter areas. Pansies do best in a rich garden loam, kept evenly moist, but not wet. Fertilize once or twice during the growing season, a month or so apart.

with darker rings. Prevalent during periods of warm, humid weather, disease can be lessened by immediately removing and disposing of any infected leaves, avoiding overhead watering, and permitting good air circulation between plants with generous spacing.

Slugs and Snails

If something has eaten major portions (or *all*) of your pansies' new growth— and has left telltale slime trails—you'll know you have slugs, snails or both. Although there are a number of more-or-less effective natural controls, even the most organic gardeners use a product called Escar-Go, which contains iron phosphate, a naturally occurring soil element (see page 145), to control these frustrating pests. Chemical controls include products (usually in bait form) containing metaldehyde or methiocarb (see page 148). Whether using Escar-Go or a chemical control, scatter it all around potential targets and any damp, shady spot where slugs and snails hide during the day. If you know there are slugs or snails in your area, always treat your garden with a control before their damage is apparent; slugs and snails can do a tremendous amount of damage in even one night.

Zinnia
ZINNIA

Annual

All Zones

Japanese Beetles

If you see holes eaten right through zinnia leaves, leaving nothing but the veins, the culprits are likely to be Japanese beetles. The beetles are metallic green or brownish and about $1/2$ inch long. Control with insecticidal soap (see page 144). Control future generations with milky spores, which kill the grubs as they overwinter in the soil (see page 150). Chemical controls include products that contain acephate, carbaryl or malathion (see pages 146 and 148).

Powdery Mildew

Thriving in hot, dry conditions, zinnias will occasionally be bothered by powdery mildew if growing conditions turn humid.

Although the disease is not fatal, its signature powdery white coating on foliage and flowers is unattractive. Remove and destroy any infected plants. Prevent further outbreaks of powdery mildew with a spray of liquid sulfur or baking soda (see pages 143 and 145). Or avoid the problem altogether by planting a mildew-resistant variety (see page 21).

Zinnia Blight

Zinnia blight causes brownish spots with gray centers to develop on all parts of zinnias, including flowers. Trim off and destroy any infected parts. Keep the problem from developing in the future by avoiding overhead watering,

watering in the morning, and spacing plants generously to increase air circulation.

Zinnias, with their vibrant colors and strong stems, make great cut flowers and sturdy, upstanding members of any flower border. Plant them in a full-sun location, in a rich, well-drained soil. Keep soil evenly moist, but not wet; feed monthly with a complete fertilizer. Avoid wetting the foliage to keep problems with mildew to a minimum.

◀ CHAPTER 4 ▶

PREVENTION GLOSSARY

Don't let the fact that a wide array of garden care products are presented on the following pages lead you to believe that you need a fully stocked arsenal to protect your plants from pests and diseases. In reality, good gardeners—those who give their plants the cultural care they need—find they need very few commercial products to maintain a healthy garden. What products you do need should always be stored with safety in mind, particularly in households with small children, and disposed of properly, whether you've used up all the product or not. Follow the advice found on pages 140-149 and you can count yourself as a good gardener and an environmentally aware citizen.

MEANS OF PREVENTION

The first rule in applying any product to the garden is to read and follow all label directions to the letter—including advice for using protective gear and/or clothing.

Throughout this book, we have ordered the solutions to your garden's pest problems from the most benign—in terms of toxicity to the environment—to the most extreme measures. In almost all cases, we think you'll find the least toxic solutions will work just fine, especially if you've followed the basics for a healthy garden, as outlined on pages 10-21.

On these pages you'll find descriptions of the various products recommended throughout this book. They are intended for general information only; in every case where you use a commercially available pesticide,

it's your responsibility—to yourself, your family, your pets and the environment—to read and follow all label instructions to the letter. This includes recommended dilution rates, application instructions and disposal instructions.

Disposing of leftover chemical pesticides presents a problem for most home gardeners—so much so that many communities have instituted special days during the year when one can bring hazardous materials to designated locations for safe disposal. Previously, many people simply poured leftover pesticides down the drain, where these extremely concentrated poisons eventually found their way into rivers, streams and aquifers. If a pest situation is severe enough to require a chemical solution, instead of buying pesticides in concentrated forms (which very few gardeners are ever able to use completely), consider buying these products in a premixed (prediluted) form. Premixed pesticides are easier to use and are sold in quantities most gardeners find easy to use up—a reasonable solution to the disposal problem.

Gardeners in households that include children should pay close attention to the products they use in their garden.

WHAT'S IN A NAME?

The following terms are used frequently in conjunction with pest control. It will help you get the product you need if you know what to ask for.

Pesticide: An agent that kills pests (generally considered to include insects, mites, slugs and snails, nematodes and diseases).

Insecticide: An agent that kills insects.

Miticide: An agent that kills mites.

Molluscicide: An agent that kills slugs and snails.

Nematicide: An agent that kills nematodes.

Fungicide: An agent that kills fungus.

More and more garden products are available in premixed forms which (because the possibility of leftover, undiluted spray is all but eliminated) are favored by those who own small- to medium-sized gardens.

Herbicide: An agent that kills herbaceous plants (generally considered a "weed killer").

When it comes time to purchase a packaged garden product, either you know exactly what you want, or you don't. If you don't, seek out qualified advice to make sure you get what you need.

TIP **WHERE TO GET ANSWERS**

If you have any questions about a pesticide you are using or are planning to use, check the telephone book for the state pesticide agency or the local office of the Environmental Protection Agency (EPA). The EPA and Texas Tech University Health Sciences Center School of Medicine have combined forces and set up the National Pesticide Telecommunications Network, a 24-hour telephone hotline which can be reached at 800-858-PEST.

Your Own Safety

No matter what type of pesticide you use, there are certain rules you must follow for safety's sake:

- **Read the label** every time you spray or dust, and note especially all the cautions and warnings. Mix sprays on a solid, level surface to avoid spillage.

- **Avoid spilling** pesticides on skin or clothing and wash exposed skin areas thoroughly with soap and water.

- **Do not eat or smoke** while spraying. Wash hands thoroughly with soap and water immediately after spraying.

- **Keep all chemicals out of the reach of children.** Store in a locked cabinet or on a high shelf. Set aside a special set of mixing tools, measuring spoons and a graduated measuring cup. Use them only for mixing and measuring chemicals. Be sure to keep all chemicals in their original labeled containers at all times.

- **Follow all label instructions** for disposal of leftover spray.

- **Unused pesticides** must be disposed of properly to avoid harming the environment. Check the guidelines of your community's hazardous materials department.

Kids are naturally attracted to all manner of life in the garden; it's the gardener's responsibility to make sure it's a safe place to explore.

HOW TOXIC IS IT?

The relative toxicity of any pesticide is indicated on the product label with one of the following words, usually in large print.

Danger = Highly toxic

Poison = Highly toxic

Warning = Moderately toxic

Caution = Slightly toxic

If the product is relatively non-toxic, no word will appear on the label.

NATURAL PESTICIDES AND FUNGICIDES

The past several years have seen a proliferation of "natural" or organic garden products. Remember, however, natural doesn't necessarily mean non-toxic: be sure to consult the label for relative toxicity levels.

Caution Still Applies

In the past generation, a great number of products have come onto the market that are seen as alternatives to synthetic pesticides and fungicides. In general, this has been a good trend, resulting both in more environmental consciousness on the part of home gardeners, and in less spraying of truly harmful products.

But one popular misconception persists: namely, that if a pesticide or fungicide is natural, it is safe. Granted, there are many natural pesticides that are not poisonous, but if the natural product is in fact a poison (such as pyrethrins derived from the chrysanthemum plant), it is just as poisonous as a synthetically produced pesticide (such as the synthetic form of pyrethrin, called pyrethoid).

Bottom line: Always read and follow all label directions and cautions to the letter, no matter what type of product you are using.

Azadirachtin

Azadirachtin is sold under the tradename Neem, Bioneem, Neem-Away, Rose Defense and others. Toxic to bees, this broad-spectrum insecticide is produced from a tropical tree called *Azadirachta indica*. The active ingredient, azadirachtin, works two

ways on insects: First, once sprayed on a plant, it keeps many insects from even landing; second, it disrupts the internal workings of a wide variety of pests, usually causing death within a few days. Azadirachtin controls aphids, beetles, caterpillars, locusts, mealybugs, spider mites and whiteflies. Interestingly, recent tests indicate azadirachtin may also work as a fungicide, controlling black spot, mildew, rust and other diseases. **Toxicity rating:** Caution.

Cucumber beetles are one of the many insects that cause double trouble — chewing the foliage of plants, then spreading a variety of diseases as they feed. Limit damage by controlling at the first sign of attack.

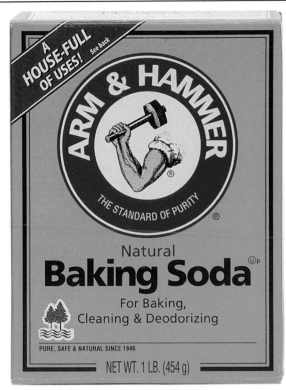

Baking soda has a number of beneficial uses in the garden, including use as a preventative for a number of plant diseases.

Bacillus popilliae

Bacillus popilliae is sold under the tradename Milky Spore, Doom and others. A special strain of bacterium that kills the white grubs of Japanese beetles.
Toxicity rating: Caution.

Bacillus thuringiensis

Bacillus thuringiensis is sold under the tradename Dipel, Thuricide, Javelin and others. Several strains of bacterium including *Bacillus thuringiensis kurstaki*, *B.t. israeliensis*, and *B. t. san diego*, each of which kills a specific pest, including caterpillars, Colorado potato beetles, European corn borers and mosquito larvae. Safe to use around humans, pets, birds and fish. Also available in granules.
Toxicity rating: Caution.

Bt or Btk granules: see *Bacillus thuringiensis*.

Baking Soda

Baking soda is sold simply as baking soda. This substance may be harmful to fish. Recent tests have shown that a simple mixture of common baking soda and water (mixed at the ratio of 4 teaspoons baking soda to 1 gallon water; if possible, $2^{1}/_{2}$ tablespoons of ultra-fine horticultural oil added to the mix will help the solution stick to foliage longer) works in preventing anthracnose, black spot and powdery mildew. Repeat spray every two weeks.
Toxicity rating: None.

Chitin

Chitin is sold under the tradename Clandosan, and is a soil amendment made up from the substance that forms the exoskeletons of insects and crustaceans. When incorporated into garden soil, chitin produces an environment that kills harmful nematodes.
Toxicity rating: Caution.

Copper Compounds

Copper compounds are sold under the tradenames Bordeaux mix, Kocide 101 and others. These are broad-spectrum fungicides and bactericides that prevent brown rot, downy mildew, fireblight, peach leaf curl and shot-hole diseases. Toxic to fish.
Toxicity rating: Caution.

Fungicidal Soap

Fungicidal soap is sold under the tradename Soap Shield. This broad-spectrum fungicide is a mixture of fixed copper and potassium salts of fatty acids derived from plants and animals. Fungicidal soap controls a wide variety of diseases including black rot, black spot, botrytis (gray mold), leaf spot and powdery mildew.
Toxicity rating: Caution.

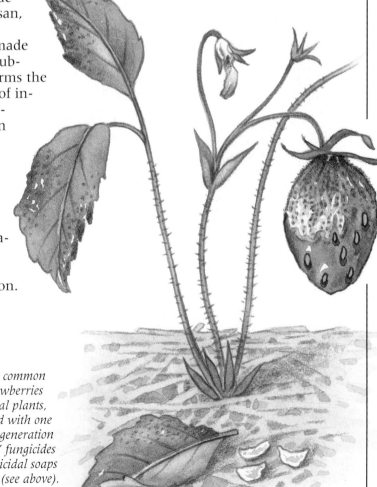

Botrytis, a common disease of strawberries and ornamental plants, can be controlled with one of the new generation "natural" fungicides known as fungicidal soaps (see above).

Horticultural oil is an old-fashioned, very effective remedy for a variety of garden maladies. It is available in two weights: a lighter weight for summer use and a heavier oil for use during periods of dormancy.

Insecticidal Soap

Insecticidal soap is sold under the tradename Safer and others. It is toxic to fish. Insecticidal soaps are mild poisons extracted from the potassium salts naturally present in the fatty acids found in animals and plants. They are effective on soft-bodied insects like aphids and spider mites, but not on hard-bodied insects like beetles. The salts enter the cell walls of the soft-bodied insects and cause death. For the soap to be effective, an insect must actually come into contact with it, so fast-flying insects that flee the spray do, in fact, get away free.

The risks from insecticidal soap—to humans, domestic animals and the environment—are very low; and it does not leave a harmful residue on edible plants. Insecticidal soap is safe to use indoors as well as outside. Some caution must still be taken with its application, however; as effective as it is against harmful soft-bodied insects, insecticidal soap also kills soft-bodied beneficial insects.
Toxicity rating: Caution.

Insecticidal soap is an effective control for a large number of insects, with very low toxicity. See above for more information.

Horticultural Oil

Horticultural oil is sold under the tradenames Sun Spray, Volck, Oil-Away and others. These products smother insects and are especially effective against aphids, lacebugs, mealybugs, scale insects, spider mites and whiteflies. There is a lightweight horticultural oil (sometimes called summer, superior or verdant oils) that can be used during the growing season, and a heavier form for use during the dormant season; do not use the heavier dormant oil spray during the growing season because it can burn, or even kill, plants. These products are toxic to fish.
Toxicity rating: Caution.

Iron Phosphate

Iron phosphate is sold under the tradename Escar-Go. It is the active ingredient in an effective slug and snail killer. Iron phosphate is safe for use around pets and wildlife; the iron phosphate breaks down and becomes part of the soil.
Toxicity rating: Caution.

Grasshoppers can wreak havoc for both farmers and home gardeners. Natural controls include Nosema locustae. *See below for more information.*

Nosema Locustae

Nosema locustae is sold under the tradenames Nosema, Grasshopper Attack and others. The microscopic protozoa kill grasshoppers and crickets. Nosema locustae is usually sold in bait form.
Toxicity rating: Caution.

Rotenone

Rotenone is sold under the tradename Rotenone. It is extremely toxic to fish, but not toxic to bees. This is one of the most powerful of all natural insecticides. It is derived from several tropical plants and works as a contact poison against many pests including caterpillars, corn

Garden sulfur, another old-fashioned remedy, is effective against a variety of diseases and insect pests.

borers, flea beetles, harlequin bugs, leaf-eating beetles, leafhoppers, scale insects, squash bugs, squash vine borers and thrips. Wear a mask when applying; rotenone may irritate skin, so wear protective clothing.
Toxicity rating: Warning.

Sulfur

Sulfur is sold as Garden Sulfur, the tradename of Safer Garden Fungicide and others. Sulfur has long been a preventative treatment for black spot, brown spot, gray mold, powdery mildew, rust and other diseases. Sulfur has also been shown to be effective in controlling aphids, scale insects, thrips and especially effective against mites.
Toxicity rating: Caution.

Garden sulfur is available in both liquid and powdered forms.

SYNTHETIC PESTICIDES AND FUNGICIDES

Aphids are a major menace in most gardens. One of the chemical products that control aphids is acephate; see below.

Some Definitions

Synthetic pesticides (what many people refer to as "chemical" pesticides) are largely the product of technology developed during World War II. These products proliferated in the home garden market during the postwar years until research indicated that some had negative long-term environmental impact. Eventually, some were completely banned by the EPA, or banned for home use.

In the descriptions that follow, the words *systemic, contact* and *broad-spectrum* are used. Systemic means the product is actually absorbed by the plant, making the plant itself toxic (which means it kills any insect that sucks or chews on the plant). Contact, as in "kills on contact," means the product kills insects when they ingest it or come in contact with it. Broad-spectrum means a product kills a wide range of pests, as opposed to a product that singles out a particular insect or group of insects.

Acephate

Acephate is sold under the tradename Orthene. It is toxic to bees and birds and cannot be used on any edible crop. This is a systemic, broad-spectrum insecticide which kills aphids, bagworms, beetles, caterpillars, fire ants, leaf miners, thrips and other insects.
Toxicity rating: Warning.

Calcium Polysulfide

Calcium polysulfide is sold under the names "lime-sulfur," dormant spray and others. It is a caustic material, causing skin damage and may cause serious eye injury (wear eye protection). It is used primarily on dormant plants to kill overwintering fungus spores and insects.
Toxicity rating: Danger.

Captan

Captan is sold under the tradename Captan. It is toxic to bees and fish and may cause serious eye injury (wear eye protection). Captan controls brown and black rot, and leaf spots.
Toxicity rating: Danger.

Carbaryl

Carbaryl is sold under the tradename Sevin. It is highly toxic to bees and fish. A broad-spectrum insecticide, it kills insects on contact (it is not systemic), including beetles, caterpillars, fleas, spittlebugs, ticks and other pests. Carbaryl also comes in granule form.
Toxicity rating: Caution.

The chemical carbaryl kills a wide range of insects on contact. It is sold under the tradename Sevin.

Carbaryl Bait or Granules
See Carbaryl.

Caterpillars of all stripes can be voracious consumers of garden plants.

Chlorothalonil
Chlorothalonil is sold under the tradename Daconil. It is toxic to fish and may cause eye and skin damage; wear protection. This broad-spectrum fungicide controls black spot, various blights, botrytis (gray mold), leaf spot, powdery mildew and scab. **Toxicity rating:** Warning.

Dimethoate
Dimethoate is sold under the tradename Cygon. It is highly toxic to fish, bees and birds and cannot be used on any edible crop. This broad-spectrum, systemic insecticide kills aphids, lace bugs, leaf miners, scale, spittlebugs and other pests. **Toxicity rating:** Warning.

Spittlebugs are unsightly and may spread disease. Dimethoate is one of the chemical insecticides which will control spittlebugs; see above.

The chemical fungicide chlorothalonil is one of the controls for the disease known as powdery mildew.

Hexakis

Hexakis is sold under the tradenames Vendex and Isotox. It is a long-lasting miticide that kills harmful mites, but does not harm beneficial ones.

Toxicity rating: Caution.

Malathion

Malathion is sold under the trade name Malathion. It is toxic to bees and fish. This broad-spectrum contact insecticide kills aphids, caterpillars, lace bugs, mealybugs, thrips and other pests.

Toxicity rating: Warning.

The disease known as rust can be controlled with the chemical fungicide mancozeb; see below.

Mancozeb

Mancozeb is sold under the tradenames Fore, Manzate and Dithane. It is toxic to fish. Mancozeb is a broad-spectrum fungicide that controls blight, leaf spot, mildew and rust.

Toxicity rating: Caution.

Maneb

Maneb is sold under the tradename Maneb. It is highly toxic to fish. Maneb is a broad-spectrum fungicide you can use to control various blights, leaf spot, mildew, rust and other diseases.

Toxicity rating: Caution.

Metaldehyde

Metaldehyde is sold under the tradenames Bug-Geta and Slug-Geta. It is highly toxic to all wildlife (and domestic pets), including birds and fish. Metaldehyde is known as a molluscicide, and it kills slugs and snails.

Toxicity rating: Caution.

A real problem in many gardens, slugs and snails can cause a great deal of damage overnight. Metaldehyde is a chemical control that will eliminate slugs and snails; see above.

Malathion is a broad-spectrum insecticide that kills on contact. For more information, see above left.

Myclobutanil

Myclobutanil is sold under the tradename Immunox. This broad-spectrum, systemic fungicide controls black spot, mildew, rust and other diseases.

Toxicity rating: Caution.

Pyrethroid

Pyrethroid is the synthetic form of the naturally occurring poison pyrethrin. It is toxic to bees, and is sold under a variety of tradenames including deltamethrin, permethrin, remethrin, sumithrin, tetramethrin and tralomethrin. Pyrethroid may be harmful to fish. It kills aphids, ants, beetles, caterpillars, fleas, houseflies, hornets, leafhoppers, mealybugs, thrips, wasps and whiteflies.

Toxicity rating: Caution.

Triforine

Triforine is sold under the tradename Funginex. Keep

Commonly called pyrethrum, painted daisy, or Persian insect flower, Chrysanthemum coccineum is the source for the naturally-occurring insecticide, pyrethrum.

pets out of treated areas. Triforine may cause serious eye damage; be sure to wear eye protection. This is a broad-spectrum systemic that controls black spot, powdery mildew, rust and other diseases.

Toxicity rating: Danger.

Pyrethroid is one of the chemical controls that will control aphids; see above.

Insecticides including the naturally-occurring insecticide pyrethrum are sold under a variety of tradenames.

BENEFICIAL INSECTS

The idea of using what are commonly called "beneficial insects" to control damaging insects has really caught on in recent years. The following "good guys" are surprisingly effective in controlling a wide variety of garden pests. To keep them in your yard, you'll have to make them feel at home. For one person's experience in creating a favorable environment for beneficial insects, read "A Balanced Approach," on pages 30-35. You may be able to find beneficial insects at your local nursery or garden center; if you have trouble locating what you need, a large number of mail-order sources exist. See page 152 for a list of suppliers.

Aphid Midges

The larvae of this tiny black fly eat aphids. In its adult form, it eats the sap or "honeydew" produced by aphids. Sold as pupae, they should be distributed on the soil or on the plants affected with aphids.

Ladybugs

Ladybugs are famous for eating large quantities of aphids, but they'll also eat mites, scales and whiteflies. As flying insects, there's no guarantee they'll stay in your garden, but because they don't fly at night, releasing

Ladybugs should be welcome in any garden: they're voracious eaters of aphids, mites and other insect pests; see pages 38-59.

Lacewing larvae are usually sold as eggs; once they hatch, they consume amazing numbers of mites, thrips, whiteflies and many other garden pests.

them in the evening increases the chances they'll stick around—at least for a while. Recommendations vary as to how many ladybugs you'll need in an average-sized garden to be effective—anywhere from one cup to one quart.

Lacewing Larvae

Lacewing larvae are voracious eaters, consuming large quantities of aphids, caterpillars, leafhoppers, mealybugs, some scales, spider mites, thrips and young whiteflies, over a period of about three weeks. Lacewings are usually sold as eggs and should be placed on plants, approximately four lacewings for every square foot of garden.

Beneficial Nematodes

Nematodes are extremely small roundworms, barely large enough to be seen without a magnifying glass. There are basically two species of beneficial nematodes: *Steinernema carpocapsae* (Sc for short) and *Heterorhabditis bacteriophora* (Hb for short), along with several strains of each. Each strain works against a specific pest; consult your supplier for proper selection and application rates. They are usually mixed with water and applied directly to garden soil. They are harmless

to earthworms, but attack hundreds of soil-borne pests including the pupae of harmful insects. Experience suggests that it's best to use only one strain of beneficial nematodes per garden plot, because different strains seem unable to coexist.

Predator Mites

Both the adult form of predator mites and their immature nymphs are effective controls against harmful types of mites, including spider mites. There is also a species of predator mite that eats thrips. Predator mites are usually shipped in the adult stage, so be sure to release them in the garden as soon as you receive them.

Parasitoid Wasps

Don't confuse these with yellow jackets or other wasps; parasitoid wasps are so tiny that four of them could fit on the head of a pin, and they don't sting. They do, however, consume large quantities of garden pests including caterpillars, cutworms and whiteflies. Several species are available, each of which consumes specific pests; consult your supplier to get the right species and for the detailed information you need to properly release these tiny wasps in your garden.

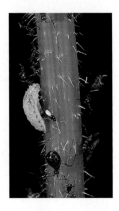

The syrphid fly larva, aphids and parasitoid wasp shown in this photograph represent the delicate balance of the insect food chain; see page 34 for more information.

SOLARIZING SOIL

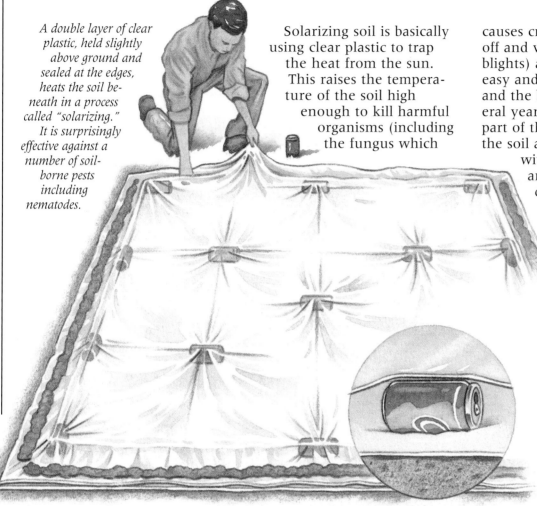

A double layer of clear plastic, held slightly above ground and sealed at the edges, heats the soil beneath in a process called "solarizing." It is surprisingly effective against a number of soilborne pests including nematodes.

Solarizing soil is basically using clear plastic to trap the heat from the sun. This raises the temperature of the soil high enough to kill harmful organisms (including the fungus which causes crown gall and damping off and various wilts and blights) and weed seeds. It's easy and surprisingly effective, and the benefits can last several years. During the hottest part of the year, start by tilling the soil and smoothing it out with a rake. Water the area well; it should be damp to a depth of 12 inches. Cover the bed with a sheet of clear plastic (from 1 to 4 mil thick). Add another layer of clear plastic, with spacers between the two (spacers can be anything from bricks to empty soda cans laid on their sides). Cover the edges of the plastic with soil. Keep the plastic in place for 4 to 8 weeks—the longer the better.

CUTWORM COLLARS

Cutworms are the larvae of several different moths. Cutworms are anywhere from 1 to 2 inches long and come in a variety of colors. These caterpillars live in the soil and do their damage at night, emerging to cut new seedlings or transplants right off at the soil line. They either retreat into the soil during the day or hide under leaves or other garden debris; if you uncover one, you'll know it's a cutworm if it is curled into its characteristic "C" shape. Although there are a number of chemical controls, one of the easiest preventative measures is to fashion a protective collar from any small metal can. Remove both the top and bottom of the can and place it over the seedling or transplant; cutworms will not be able to crawl over this barrier. Another preventative measure is to keep garden beds free of debris, which eliminates their favorite hiding places.

A tuna can, with both the top and bottom cut out, deters cutworms.

SOURCE LIST

The first place to look for garden supplies and pest control products is your local nursery or garden center. Recent years have seen dramatic improvements in the local availability of not just the standard products, but of alternatives as well. If you have trouble finding what you need locally, the following mail-order supply companies offer excellent selections of pest and disease control products. All information was accurate as of press time.

Arbico
Box 4247 CRB
Tucson, AZ 85738
800/827-2847
www.arbico.com
arbico@aol.com
Catalog: no charge

The Beneficial Insect Company
244 Forrest Street
Fort Mill, SC 20715-2325
803/547-2301
www.bugfarm.com

Biofac
P.O. Box 87
Mathis, TX 78368
800/233-4914

Bio Ag Supply
710 South Columbia
Plainview, TX 79072
800/746-9900
wwinters@texasonline.net
Catalog: no charge

Bountiful Gardens
18001 Shafer Ranch Road
Willits, CA 95490
707/459-6410

Bozeman Bio-Tech
1612 Gold Avenue
Bozeman, MT 59715
800/289-6656
www.planetnatural.com
Catalog: no charge

The Bug Store
113 West Argonne
St. Louis, MO 63122
800/455-2847
www.bugstore.com
Catalog: no charge

Eden Organic Nursery Services
P.O. Box 4604
Hallandale, FL 33008
954/455-0229
www.conseed.com
Catalog: no charge

Gardener's Supply Company
128 Intervale Road
Burlington, VT 05401
800/444-6417
www.gardeners.com
Catalog: no charge

Gardens Alive!
5100 Schenley Place
Lawrenceburg, IN 47025
812/537-8650
gardener@gardens-alive.com
Catalog: no charge

Harmony Farm Supply & Nursery
P.O. Box 460
Graton, CA 95444
707/823-9125
www.harmonyfarm.com
Catalog: no charge at bulk mailing, otherwise $2.00

Home Harvest Garden Supply
3712 Eastern Avenue
Baltimore, MD 21224
800/348-4769
www.homeharvest.com

Integrated Fertility Management
333 Ohme Gardens Road
Wenatchee, WA 98801
800/332-3179

Natural Gardening Company
217 San Anselmo Avenue
San Anselmo, CA 94960
415/456-5060
www.naturalgardening.com

Nature's Control
P.O. Box 35
Medford, OR 97501
541/899-8318
bugsnc@teleport.com
Catalog: no charge

Nitron Industries, Inc.
P.O. Box 1447
Fayetteville, AR 72702
800/835-0123
www.nitron.com
Catalog: no charge

Peaceful Valley Farm Supply
P.O. Box 2209
Grass Valley, CA 95945
530/272-4769
www.groworganic.com
Catalog: free once a year mailing, otherwise $2.00

Ringer Corporation
9959 Valley View Road
Eden Prairie, MN 55344
800/654-1047

Rohde's Nursery and Nature Store
1651 Wall Street
Garland, TX 75041
800/864-4445
www.beorganic.com
Catalog: posted on Internet only

Worm's Way
7850 Highway 37 N
Bloomington, IN 47404-9477
800/274-9676
www.wormsway.com
Catalog: no charge

PLANT HARDINESS ZONE MAP

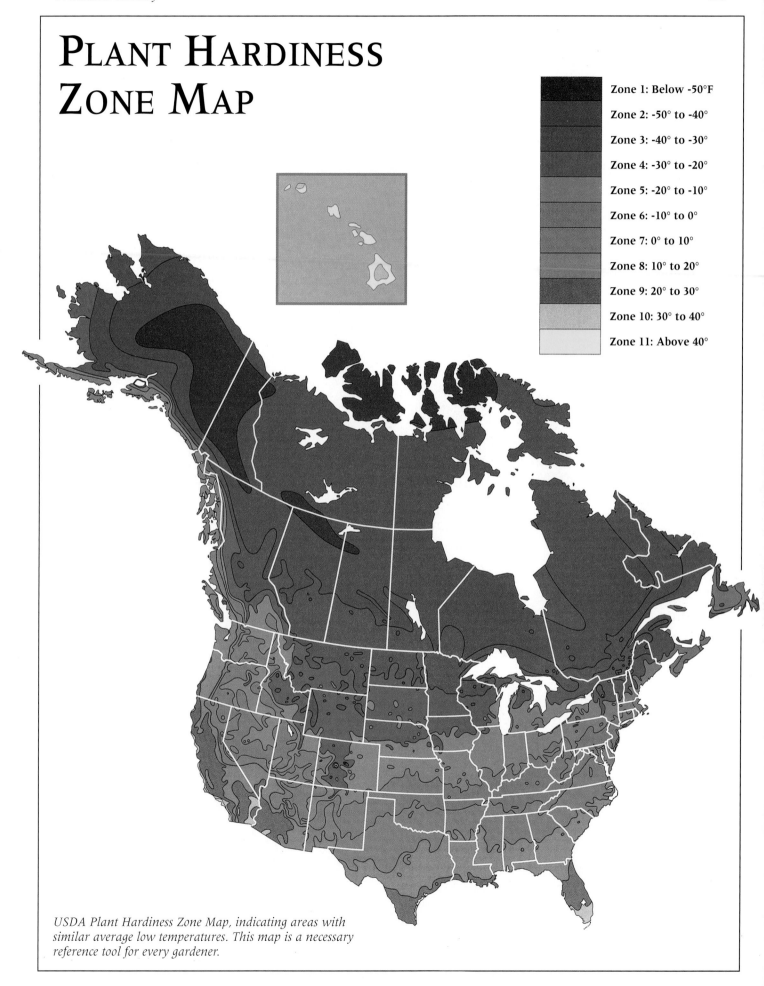

Zone 1: Below -50°F
Zone 2: -50° to -40°
Zone 3: -40° to -30°
Zone 4: -30° to -20°
Zone 5: -20° to -10°
Zone 6: -10° to 0°
Zone 7: 0° to 10°
Zone 8: 10° to 20°
Zone 9: 20° to 30°
Zone 10: 30° to 40°
Zone 11: Above 40°

USDA Plant Hardiness Zone Map, indicating areas with similar average low temperatures. This map is a necessary reference tool for every gardener.

INDEX OF PLANTS

A

African daisy, 69
Ageratum, 27, 58, 62-63
Alyssum, 34, 46, 48, 50, 52, 54, 56, 57, 59, 88, 102, 109, 134
Anemone, 38
    Anemone, Japanese, 25, 27, 65-66
Artemisia, 70
Asparagus, 35
Asparagus fern, 27
Aster, 20, 21, 72-73
Astilbe, 74-75
Azalea, 17, 23

B

Baby's breath, 97
Begonia, 27, 76-77
Bellflower, Serbian, 25
Black-eyed Susan, 128
Bleeding heart, 93
Broccoli, 34
Butterfly bush, 26
Butterfly weed, 71

C

Calendula, 42, 57, 58, 78
Camellia, 17, 31
Candytuft, 45, 103
Canna, 41, 79
Carnation, 42, 45, 57
Celosia, 80
Centaurea, 81-82
Centranthus, 25

Chrysanthemum, 38, 83-84
Cleome, 85
Coleus, 85
Columbine, 43, 69
Coneflower, 17, 94
Coralbells, 25, 27, 100
Cornflower, 38
Cosmos, 38, 87
Crepe myrtle, 21
Crocus, 88

D

Daffodil, 25, 53, 89, 112
Dahlia, 34
Daphne, 17
Datura, 58
Daylily, 9
Delphinium, 90-91
Dianthus, 39, 92
Dill, 38, 40, 50, 52, 54, 56, 57, 59
Dusty miller, 130

E

Eggplants, 35
Euryops, 27

F

Fennel, 27
Forget-me-not, 111
Foxglove, 27, 46, 94
Fuchsia, 35

G

Gardenia, 17
Gaura, 26, 27
Geranium, 40, 42, 46, 57, 58, 118-120
    Geranium, ivy, 27
Gladiolus, 34, 47, 48, 96
Gopher plant, 28
Grape hyacinth, 25

H

Hollyhock, 64
Hop bush, 25
Hosta, 101
Hyacinth, 38, 102-103

I

Impatiens, 104
Iris, 21, 24, 25, 27, 38, 45, 49, 105

J

Jasmine, star, 25
Juniper, 23, 27

L

Lantana, 25-26, 27
Larkspur, 41
Lavender, 42
    Lavender, English, 27
    Lavender, Spanish, 27

Lilac, 21
Lily, 52, 58, 107
Lily-of-the-Nile, 25, 27
Lily-of-the-valley, 86
Lion's tail, 26
Lobelia, 108
Lupine, 110

M

Mâche, 34
Maple, Japanese, 27
Marigold, 34, 131-132

N

Narcissus, 27, 53
Nasturtium, 42, 45, 133
Neem tree, 142
Nicotiana, 58, 113

O

Oleander, 27
Oregano, 27

P

Pansy, 59, 137
Pennisetum, 27
Penstemon, 26, 27, 58, 121
Peony, 54, 115-116
Petunia, 58, 122-123
Phlox, 21, 53, 124
Plumbago, 25
Poinsettia, 57
Poppy, 117
Potato vine, 25

Q

Queen Anne's lace, 38, 40

R

Redwood, 25
Rhododendron, 17
Rockrose, 25, 27
Rose, 21, 23, 34, 35, 39, 40,
    46, 47, 55, 56, 125-127
Rosemary, 27

S

Sage, 27
    Sage, Mexican, 27
Scabiosa, 46, 48, 56, 88,
    102, 134
Sea lavender, 25, 27
Sedum, 25, 129
Snapdragon, 17, 21, 67-68
Sunflower, 57, 98
Sweet pea, 106

T

Thyme, 27
Tomato, 35, 58
Tulip, 23, 58, 134

V

Verbena, 135
Veronica, 136
Violet, 59

Y

Yarrow, 25, 27, 38, 40, 46,
    54, 62

Z

Zinnia, 21, 34, 137

GENERAL INDEX

A

Acephate, 38, 40, 46, 48, 50, 51, 52, 57, 58, 59, 62, 63, 64, 65, 67, 69, 70, 71, 72, 73, 74, 75, 76, 77, 78, 79, 81, 82, 83, 84, 85, 87, 89, 90, 92, 95, 96, 97, 98, 99, 102, 104, 106, 107, 108, 110, 111, 113, 116, 117, 118, 119, 121, 122, 125, 126, 128, 129, 131, 132, 133, 134, 135, 136, 137, 146

Anthracnose, 46, 68, 94, 115

Ants, 38, 70, 72, 74, 76, 78, 81, 85, 87, 101, 116, 129

Ants, fire, 34, 146, 147

Aphids, 30, 31, 33, 38, 53, 55, 67, 69, 70, 72, 74, 76, 78, 81, 83, 85, 87, 92, 96, 98, 99, 102, 104, 107, 108, 110, 117, 120, 121, 122, 125, 127, 129, 131, 134, 135, 142, 144, 145, 146, 147, 148, 149, 150

Aphids, bean, 133

Aphids, brown ambrosia, 128

Aphids, foxglove, 136

Aphids, geranium, 119

Aphids, green peach, 111

Aster yellows, 38, 69, 73, 82, 83, 87, 97, 108, 109, 128, 131

Azadirachtin, 38, 42, 50, 53, 58, 62, 65, 67, 69, 70, 72, 75, 77, 81, 83, 84, 85, 89, 90, 94, 96, 99, 102, 104, 105, 107, 108, 110, 111, 113, 116, 117, 118, 119, 120, 121, 122, 124, 125, 126, 127, 128, 129, 131, 133, 134, 135, 136, 142

B

Bagworms, 146

Baking soda, 143

Baking soda spray, 54, 62, 73, 75, 89, 125, 127, 128, 135, 136, 137

Bees, 142, 146, 147, 148, 149

Beetles, 142, 146, 147, 149

Beetle, asparagus, 33

Beetle, black blister, 65

Beetle, blister, 40

Beetle, Colorado potato, 43, 113, 122, 143

Beetle, cucumber, 39, 123

Beetle, flea, 35, 39, 145

Beetle, fuller rose, 47, 126

Beetle, ground, 44, 56

Beetle, Japanese, 34, 50, 64, 72, 75, 79, 85, 89, 95, 116, 126, 132, 137, 143

Beetle, leaf-eating, 145

Beetle, potato flea, 111, 114, 123, 133

Beetle, red lily leaf, 107

Beetle, soldier, 38, 44, 48

Beetle, spotted cucumber, 79, 87, 104

Beetle, sunflower, 98

Benomyl, 112

Bird netting, 23, 26, 27

Birds, 27, 56, 58

Black spot, 39, 125, 142, 143, 145, 147, 149

Blight, 147, 148, 151

Blight, bacterial, 117

Blight, phytophthora, 54, 116

Blight, ray, 84

Blight, southern, 68, 82, 86, 121, 124, 129, 130, 132

Blight, zinnia, 137

Bordeaux mixture, 45, 125

Borer, 49, 96, 107, 126

Borer, burdock, 41

Borer, columbine, 43, 69

Borer, corn, 46, 89, 143, 145

Borer, iris, 105

Borer, squash vine, 145

Borer, stalk, 43, 91

Boron, 15

Brown spot, 145

Bt, 42, 43, 44, 45, 46, 51, 55, 58, 62, 65, 68, 69, 89, 91, 92, 98, 103, 108, 113, 118, 121, 122, 126, 133, 136, 143

Budworms, 35

Budworms, rose, 55, 126

Butterfly, Chalcedon checkerspot, 136

C

Cabbage loopers, 118, 133

Cabbageworms, imported, 133

Calcium, 15

Calcium polysulfide, 146

Canker, brown, 40, 125

Captan, 146

Carbaryl, 40, 42, 43, 44, 46, 48, 50, 51, 57, 58, 62, 64,

65, 66, 67, 70, 72, 73, 75,
77, 78, 79, 81, 82, 84, 85,
87, 89, 95, 96, 97, 100,
104, 106, 108, 111, 113,
114, 116, 117, 118, 119,
121, 122, 123, 126, 128,
132, 133, 137, 146

Carbon, 15

Caterpillars, 42, 118, 142,
143, 145, 146, 147, 148,
149, 150

    Caterpillar, monarch, 71

    Caterpillar, woollybear,
68, 98, 122

Cercospora leaf spot, 42

Chickens, 56

Chitin, 68, 80, 85, 89, 103,
104, 109, 112, 116, 120,
123, 124, 143

Chlorine, 15

Chlorothalonil, 39, 45, 46,
49, 52, 63, 67, 70, 73, 81,
83, 115, 147

Cobalt, 15

Copper, 15, 45, 143

Copper spray, 136

Copper strips, 56

Copper sulfate, 76, 90, 92,
118

Crown gall, 44, 97, 151

Crows, 23

Cutworms, 44, 65, 92, 108,
113, 150

D

Damping off, 44, 106, 151

Deer, 22-27

Deer repellents, 26

Deficiency, iron, 49

Didymellina leaf spot, 45

Dimethoate, 69, 71, 82, 96,
147

Disease-resistant plants, 21

Dodder, 122-123

Dormant oil spray, 35

Ducks, 56

E

Earwigs, 45, 89, 131

Earworms, corn, 62

F

Fasciation, bacterial, 106,
122

Fences, 23-27

    Fences, electric, 24

Fertilizer, 14-17

    Fertilizer, types, 16

Fertilizing annuals, 17

Fertilizing evergreens, 17

Fertilizing perennials, 17

Fertilizing vegetables, 17

Fireblight, 143

Fleas, 146, 147, 149

Fungicidal soap, 143

Fungicide, 140

G

Gophers, 28-29

Grasshoppers, 48, 65, 70,
145

Gray mold (Botrytis), 83,
96, 102, 106, 107, 111,
115, 118, 126, 131

Grubs, white, 147

H

Harlequin bugs, 145

Herbicide, 140

Hexakis, 64, 84, 124, 127,
132, 134, 135, 148

Honeydew, 38, 70, 72, 74,
76, 78, 81, 85, 87, 101,
116, 127, 129, 150

Horticultural oil, 51, 55, 56,
57, 59, 63, 64, 65, 68, 72,
73, 74, 82, 83, 87, 108,
119, 120, 124, 127, 128,
132, 135, 144

Housefly, 149

Hydrogen, 15

I

Insecticidal soap, 46, 50, 51,
52, 53, 55, 57, 59, 62, 63,
64, 65, 67, 68, 69, 70, 72,
73, 74, 76, 77, 78, 79, 80,
81, 82, 83, 85, 87, 89, 90,
91, 92, 94, 95, 96, 97, 98,
99, 100, 102, 103, 104,
105, 107, 108, 110, 111,
112, 115, 116, 117, 119,
120, 121, 123, 124, 125,
127, 128, 129, 131, 132,
133, 134, 135, 136, 137,
144

Insecticide, 140

Insects, beneficial, 32, 34

Iron, 15

Iron phosphate, 56, 66, 75,
77, 78, 86, 91, 93, 97,
101, 105, 116, 120, 123,
132, 137, 150, 154

L

Lace bugs, 50, 72, 83, 101,
144, 147, 148

Lacewing, 34, 38, 48, 55,
93, 116, 127, 129, 150

Ladybugs, 38, 55, 150

Leaf curl, peach, 143

Leaf scorch, 52

Leaf spot, 52, 64, 69, 73, 80, 84, 85, 92, 100, 108, 110, 113, 116, 121, 136, 137, 143, 146, 147, 148

Leaf spot, bacterial, 76

Leafhoppers, 51, 55, 65, 73, 82, 92, 97, 107, 108, 117, 120, 127, 128, 131, 132, 145, 150

Leafminers, 51, 71, 83, 90, 146, 147

   Leafminers, columbine, 69

   Leafminers, serpentine, 133

   Leafminers, verbena, 135

Leafroller, 51, 62, 67, 79, 106, 108, 119, 132

Leaftier, 62, 67, 82, 106, 119, 132

Lime, 47, 52

Locusts, 142

Loopers, cabbage, 42

M

Macronutrients, 15, 16

Magnesium, 15

Malathion, 38, 40, 46, 48, 50, 51, 52, 57, 59, 63, 64, 66, 67, 69, 70, 72, 73, 75, 76, 77, 78, 79, 81, 82, 83, 84, 85, 87, 89, 90, 95, 96, 97, 98, 99, 100, 102, 104, 107, 108, 110, 111, 116, 117, 119, 121, 125, 126, 128, 129, 131, 132, 133, 134, 135, 136, 137, 148

Mancozeb, 67, 73, 116, 148

Maneb, 63, 81, 148

Manganese, 15

Mealybugs, 52, 77, 85, 100, 119, 142, 144, 148, 150

Metaldehyde, 56, 66, 75, 77, 78, 86, 91, 93, 97, 101, 105, 116, 120, 123, 132, 137, 148

Methiocarb, 56, 66, 75, 77, 78, 86, 91, 93, 97, 101, 105, 116, 120, 123, 132, 137

Methoxychlor, 111, 114, 123, 133

Mice, 29

Midge, aphid, 150

Mildew, 35, 142, 148, 149

   Mildew, downy, 45, 81, 113, 136, 143

   Mildew, powdery, 54, 62, 73, 75, 78, 82, 84, 89, 95, 98, 100, 103, 106, 110, 114, 117, 124, 126-127, 128, 130, 135, 136, 137, 143, 145, 147

Milky spore, 50, 64, 72, 75, 79, 89, 95, 116, 123, 126, 132, 137, 143

Mites, 148, 150

   Mites, bronze, 35

   Mites, bulb, 41, 88, 96, 102, 134

   Mites, cyclamen, 90

   Mites, fuchsia, 35

   Mites, predator, 150

   Mites, spider, 57, 62, 68, 80, 84, 87, 91, 92, 99, 104, 120, 124, 127, 132, 134, 135, 142, 144, 145, 150

   Mites, two-spotted spider, 64

Miticide, 140

Mold, gray (Botrytis), 49, 63, 143, 145, 147

Mold, sooty, 70, 74, 76, 78, 81, 85

Moles, 28-29

Moluscicide, 140

Molybdenum, 15

Mosaic, rose, 55

Mosquito, 143

Moth, diamondback, 45, 103

Moth, gypsy, 34

Moth, plume, 118

Myclobutanil, 67, 149

N

Narcissus bulb flies, 107, 112

Narcissus streak, 53

Neem, 48, 59, 142

Nematicide, 140

Nematodes, 54, 71, 89, 99, 124, 143

   Nematodes, beneficial, 44, 47, 49, 51, 59, 65, 69, 72, 74, 76, 81, 83, 87, 89, 91, 100, 104, 105, 108, 123, 126, 133, 135, 150

   Nematodes, bulb, 103

   Nematodes, parasitic, 40

   Nematodes, southern root-knot, 68, 80, 85, 103, 104, 109, 112, 116, 120, 123

   Nematodes, spring dwarf, 77

   Nematodes, stem, 103, 112

Nematrol, 68, 80, 85, 89, 99, 103, 104, 109, 112, 116, 120, 123, 124

Nickel, 15

Nitrogen, 15, 16

Nosema locustae, 48, 145

Nutrients, 15

O

Oedema, 53
Oil sprays, 46
Organic matter, 10
Oxygen, 15

P

Parasitoid flies, 51
Pesticide, 140
Pest-resistant plants, 22-29
Phlox plant bugs, 53, 124
Phosphorus, 15, 16
Plant bugs, four-lined, 46, 115, 117
Potassium, 15, 16
Pyrethrin, 38, 70, 79, 81, 87, 104, 111, 113, 114, 122, 123, 133, 142
Pyrethroid, 149, 142
Pyrethrum, 40, 42, 50, 51, 56, 57, 58, 59, 65, 77

R

Rabbits, 26
Raccoons, 23, 24
Raised beds, 28-29
Rose leaf curl, 55
Rose midges, 55, 127
Rot, basal, 39, 112
Rot, black stem, 40
Rot, black, 143, 146
Rot, brown, 143, 146
Rot, bud, 41
Rot, bulb, 41
Rot, canna bud, 41, 79
Rot, crown, 101, 111
Rot, dry, 88, 96
Rot, fusarium bulb, 47
Rot, root, 13, 54, 77, 108, 109, 114, 129
Rot, soft, 38, 99, 102, 105

Rot, stem, 57, 93, 100, 132
Rot, Texas root, 95
Rotenone, 42, 46, 50, 51, 58, 59, 65, 81, 89, 113, 122, 145
Row covers, 26, 35
Rust, 56, 64, 66, 67, 70, 73, 82, 84, 92, 98, 100, 110, 119, 127, 128, 129, 130, 136, 142, 145, 148, 149

S

Salamanders, 56
Scab, 147
Scale, 35, 56, 82, 93, 101, 116, 129, 144, 145, 147
Selecting plants, 18-21
Shot-hole disease, 143
Skunks, 23
Slugs, 56, 66, 75, 77, 78, 86, 91, 93, 97, 101, 105, 116, 120, 123, 132, 137, 145, 148
Slugs, bristly rose, 40, 125
Snails, 34, 56, 66, 75, 77, 78, 86, 91, 93, 97, 101, 105, 116, 120, 123, 132, 137, 145, 148
Snapdragon leaf spot, 68
Soil amendments, 11
Soil test, 11
Soil, clay, 12
Soil, loam, 12
Soil, sand, 13
Soil, solarizing, 58, 68, 80, 82, 85, 86, 89, 97, 99, 103, 104, 106, 109, 112, 116, 117, 120, 122, 123, 124, 130, 132, 151
Spittlebug, 57, 146, 147
Squash bugs, 145
Squirrel, 25, 27
Stink bugs, 44

Streptomycin, 76, 90, 92, 118
Sulfur, 15, 45, 52, 56, 145
Sulfur spray, 35, 62, 64, 66, 67, 73, 75, 84, 92, 98, 100, 103, 106, 110, 113, 114, 117, 119, 121, 127, 128, 129, 130, 135, 136, 137
Syrphid flies, 34, 38, 55

T

Tachinid flies, 44, 81
Tarnished plant bugs, 57, 89, 96, 98, 104, 132
Thrips, 35, 62, 64, 77, 84, 94, 99, 105, 127, 145, 146, 148, 150
Thrips, gladiolus, 48, 96
Ticks, 146, 147
Toads, 56
Tobacco budworms, 58, 62, 118, 121, 122
Tomato hornworms, 58
Trichlorfon, 107, 112
Triforine, 70, 114, 149

V

Violet sawflies, 59
Virus, 84, 92, 107, 120, 127
Virus, cucumber mosaic, 122, 134
Virus, mosaic, 53
Virus, narcissus mosaic, 112
Virus, ornithogalum mosaic, 103
Virus, tobacco mosaic, 114
Virus, tulip breaking, 58, 134
Voles, 29

W

Wasps, 38, 149
  Wasps, beneficial, 65, 93, 101, 116, 127, 129
  Wasps, parasitic, 40, 46, 48, 52, 62, 126, 150
  Wasps, parasitoid, 44, 58, 81

Wasps, trichogramma, 51
Watering, 12-13
  Watering, depth, 13
Weevil, 59
  Weevil, black vine, 74, 76
  Weevil, strawberry root, 100
Whiteflies, 31, 33, 59, 63, 77, 78, 85, 110, 135, 142, 144, 149, 150
Wilt, 132, 151
  Wilt, bacterial, 39, 104, 133
  Wilt, fusarium, 47, 74, 94
  Wilt, verticillium, 58, 94, 117
Wireworms, 108
Worms, fall web, 46, 126

Y

Yellows, fusarium, 47

Z

Zinc, 15
Zineb, 73

Photo/Illustration Credits

Photographers

Jim Block: pp. cover, 2-3, 14, 17, 20, 21, 22, 23, 24(2), 25, 26(2), 27(2), 28, 32, 63, 64, 72, 73, 84, 86, 87, 88, 90, 93, 98, 100, 111, 117(2), 123, 126, 127, 129, 132, 134, 137, 140, 141, 149; **Bill Johnson:** pp. 1, 4, 21(2), 25, 33, 35(2), 36-37, 68 both, 69, 70, 71, 82, 85, 92, 93, 100, 101(2), 105, 113, 116, 120, 121, 124, 125, 127(2), 128, 134, 135, 142, 145, 146, 147(3), 148(2), 150 all; **Walter Chandoha:** pp. 4, 6, 8-9, 10, 12, 13, 15, 17, 18 both, 19, 22, 23(2), 24(2), 26, 29, 65, 74, 76, 77, 87, 88, 95, 97, 98, 104, 105, 107, 110, 112, 114, 115, 119, 122, 133, 140, 141; **Barbara and Chuck Crandall:** pp. 10(2), 11 both, 13, 16(2), 17, 19, 27, 29, 60-61, 62, 66, 67, 69, 70, 75, 77, 78, 79, 80, 83, 86, 91, 94, 95, 96, 98, 99, 101, 102, 103, 105, 106, 109, 112, 121, 122, 130, 131, 133, 136, 137; ©**Alan & Linda Detrick:** pp. 12, 13, 14, 16, 17(2), 21(3), 31, 33, 140, 142; **Derek Fell:** pp. 12, 14, 16, 19, 28, 29, 64, 71, 80, 81, 85, 87, 88, 97, 99, 103, 104, 110, 114, 115, 117, 118, 123, 126, 130, 138-139; **Rosalind Creasy:** pp. 30 both, 31, 32, 34; **Becky & Brent's Bulbs:** p. 89; **Michael Landis:** pp. 91, 94, 108, 123, 125; ©**John Mowers/Mowers Photography:** pp. 143, 144 both, 145(2), 146, 147, 148, 149(2).

Illustrators

Bill Reynolds/K&K Studios: pp. 11, 15, 38 all, 39(2), 41(2), 43(2), 44 all, 45(2), 47(2), 48, 49, 50 both, 51 all, 52 (2), 53, 54, 55(2), 56 all, 57(3), 58(3), 59(2), 90, 143, 151 both; **Debra Moloshok:** pp. 39, 40, 41, 42 all, 45(2), 46(3), 47, 48, 52, 53, 54(3), 67, 73, 84, 88, 112, 119, 125; **Greg Copeland/K&K Studios:** pp. 40(3), 41, 43, 46, 47, 49(2), 53(2), 55(2), 57, 58, 59, 106, 116